D0359027

RTC Limerick

3 9002 00027480 4

Marketing the Unknown

To
Pascale
Clément, Renaud, Maxence, Arthur

Marketing the Unknown

Developing Market Strategies for Technical Innovations

PAUL MILLIER

Professor of Industrial Marketing at E.M. **LYON** (France)
Visiting Professor at Cranfield School of Management (UK)

JOHN WILEY & SONS, LTD

Chichester · New York · Weinheim · Brisbane · Singapore · Toronto

Previously published 1997 by Dunod, Paris under the title "Stratégie et Marketing de l'Innovation Technologique"

English language Copyright © 1999 by John Wiley & Sons Ltd,
Baffins Lane, Chichester,
West Sussex PO19 1UD, England

National   01243 779777
International (+ 44) 1243 779777
e-mail (for orders and customer service enquiries):
cs-books@wiley.co.uk
Visit our Home Page on http://www.wiley.co.uk
or http://www.wiley.com

All Right Reserved. No part of this publication may be reproduced, stored in a retrieval system, or transmitted, in any form or by any means, electronic, mechanical, photocopying, recording, scanning or otherwise, except under the terms of the Copyright, Designs and Patents Act 1988 or under the terms of a licence issued by the Copyright Licensing Agency, 90 Tottenham Court Road, London, UK W1P 9HE, without the permission in writing of the publisher.

Other Wiley Offices

John Wiley & Sons, Inc. 605 Third Avenue,
New York, NY 10158–0012, USA

WILEY-VCH Verlag GmbH, Pappelallee 3,
D-69469 Weinheim, Germany

Jacaranda Wiley Ltd, 33 Park Road, Milton,
Queensland 4064, Australia

John Wiley & Sons (Asia) Pte Ltd, 2 Clementi Loop #02–01,
Jin Xing Distripark, Singapore 129809

John Wiley & Sons (Canada) Ltd, 22 Worcester Road,
Rexdale, Ontario M9W 1L1, Canada

Limerick Institute of Technology - LIBRARY
Institiúid Teicneolaíochta Luimnigh - LEABHARLANN
Class No.   658.8 MIL
ACC.NO.   19802
Date:

Library of Congress Cataloging-in-Publication Data
Millier, Paul,
[Stratégie et marketing de l'innovation technologique. English]
Marketing the unknown : developing market strategies for technical innovations / Paul Millier.
p.   cm.
Originally published in French by Dunod (Paris), 1997.
Includes bibliographical references and index.
ISBN 0-471-98621-6 (alk. paper)
1. New products—Marketing.   2. Product management.   I. Title.
HF5415. 153.M55413   1999
658.8–dc21   99–13345
CIP

British Library Cataloguing in Publication Data

A catalogue record for this book is available from the British Library

ISBN 0-471-98621-6

Typset in BookEns Ltd, Royston, Herts.
Printed and bound in Great Britain by Bookcraft (Bath) Ltd, Midsomer Norton, Somerset.

This book is printed on acid-free paper responsibly manufactured from sustainable forestry, in which at least two trees are planted for each one used for paper production.

Contents

Acknowledgements

My thanks go to all the people I have had the opportunity to collaborate with from industry over the last ten years or so. They have given me the most valuable help that a researcher could wish for: a field of observation and a field of action. Among these, I should like to mention Alcatel-Cables, Bertin, the Canon Research Centre France SA, the CEA, EDF, ELF-Atochem, Framatome, Hutchinson, Kermel (joint venture between Rhone-Poulenc and Amoco Fiber), Renault Automation, the Saint-Gobain Group, Schlumberger Industries, Schneider Electric SA, Thomson-CSF, and the team from Novacité (which helps businesses to start up in the Lyon area).

I particularly wish to thank Dr Kazuya Matsumoto, President of the Canon Research Centre France SA, Mr Marc-Henri Fermont, European Vice-President of Dow Italia SPA, Ms Agathe Massat, Manager, Corporate Risk Management, of Motorola and Mr Jean-Robert Passemard, Executive Vice-President, Product and Marketing, Renault-Automation, for the moral support that they gave me concerning this book. I should like to express my gratitude to E.M. **LYON**, where I am very proud to continue working. The school has provided a stimulating and fulfilling background for my work for many years now. I wish to thank the FNEGE (Fondation Nationale pour l'Enseignement de la Gestion) for the support it brings to E.M. **LYON** in general, and to my international research work in particular. I also wish to thank Robert Salle for patiently rereading the original manuscript and for his precious advice at all levels.

My warmest thanks go to Lindsay Reid and Jean-Robert Passemard for the English translation of this book. The interest they showed in it and their undaunted commitment far exceeded my expectations. An exceptional effort was made to put the original ideas as faithfully as possible into palatable English.

Finally, I heartily thank John Wiley & Sons, Ltd, and in particular Claire Plimmer, my editor, who supported the translation project and thus made it possible for English-speaking readers to discover a small fragment of French managerial literature.

Introduction

Innovations still remain exceptional events in company life and they tend to stay in the hands of technicians or design offices. That may be an administrative problem or an necessary evil, but it signifies that innovations are peripheral to the main business and people don't know how to manage them.

Fortunately, some companies have realized the strategic importance of innovations. Take 3M, for instance. One of their major company objectives in 1993 was to generate 30% of their income from products that had been introduced on the market over the previous four years. This means, of course, that 3M's competitors have to follow the same rhythm if they don't want to be off the market in less than 10 years from now. Technical reviews and management reviews are constantly reminding us about the vital role of innovation and the relentless acceleration of progress in technology.

But although they have been saying the same thing for the last 30 years (in 1970 it was the Concorde, microprocessors, fast breeder reactors), we're still throwing away just as much public and private money on Research and Development. In 1971 Booz, Allen & Hamilton claimed that 70% of the funds devoted to R&D were devoted to failures. That's the equivalent of several billion pounds for a European country. In 1995, C.O. Clugston said $20 billion a year were wasted this way.

Some of these failures are accountable to technology (between 20% and 40% of them according to different writers), and you can't always do anything about that. For instance, tubular monoelectrodes in combustion piles thwart all attempts to model them and produce a current. The rest of those failures (75% in high-tech according to Clugston, 1995) are attributable to inadequacies in the marketing function.

This is why innovation marketing and management have inspired a lot of varied literature on the subject. Yet it isn't always exploitable in day-to-day life for all that. On the one hand, you find very rich, stimulating literature on philosophy and sociology in innovation. But it's too conceptual to be applicable. And then in parallel you get more simplistic literature that gives you the "right" recipes for succeeding (or not failing).

What you find between is new product marketing. This is presented as a rather mechanical, non-specific form of marketing that's applied at the very beginning of a product life-cycle. Checklisting is a basic tool with authors here and the process is strictly linear and methodical. It tends to give a very reductive picture of the different phases of innovation development.

Checklists (which are lists of the right questions to ask yourself if you want to succeed), the success/failure factor approach or universal success laws (PIMS:[1] Peters and Waterman, 1982; Buzzel and Gale, 1987) are all very tempting methods because they're simple and the statistics make them reassuring. But you can't escape the fact that they reduce reality to an off-the-peg list that really isn't very helpful. The fact is that nobody knows exactly how to market innovations.

What this book attempts to do is to find new answers to these innovation problems, on the grounds that each problem is unique and that there isn't necessarily a known recipe for it or a success story that corresponds. The book was also conceived to encourage constructive thinking and stimulate the imagination so that readers realize there are other possible solutions, better ones, than those they had in mind.

It's also intended to discourage "cottonwool language", to fight approximations and rudimentary analysis. "You have to go and see the customers" isn't a strategy, even if strategy does sooner or later lead you to go and see the customers.

---

[1]   The PIMS (Profit Impact of Marketing Strategy) is a research programme of the Strategic Planning Institute.

The best way to combat approximation is to force yourself to give a written form to your ideas. When you draw up a plan of what's going to happen you gradually collect the different parts of the jigsaw puzzle. But the only way to see whether any parts are missing is to assemble them. That's when you identify the loopholes in your strategy.

If you don't have a model of some kind, a basic picture of what you're aiming for, then you don't have a strategy. But you don't have a strategy either if you don't refer back constantly to what you've already done and if you don't keep remodelling as you go along. Giving form to the process is a way to visualize your strategy as an actual plan of action. It's a tangible tool for communicating and sharing that strategy. Sharing the strategy is essential if you're not alone on the project. As for communication, it's necessary as soon as you start collaborating with commercial staff, partners in industry, shareholders. It reassures the financiers and it helps industrial partners and commercial staff to act in coherence with everybody else.

Marketing doesn't have a satisfactory answer for this problem because, first and foremost, it's designed to manage products that are already commercialized. It's perfectly applicable when there are products to manage and markets to analyse but soon reveals its limitations when product definition is still rather hazy and the market too young. How do you market personal computers when you don't know who's going to buy them and what they will be used for?

Maybe the marketing literature brings some suitable answers for consumer products but it's ineffectual as far as industrial products go (that is, industrial products for other companies or organizations). The aim of this book is to counter that inadequacy by bringing a complement to industrial marketing theory as it stands and giving companies the means to launch products successfully. *Products that don't exist yet on markets that don't exist yet either.*

The book gives an important place to technology within the marketing context. It recommends a series of concrete actions, actions that were derived from observing a large number of industrial innovation projects over a long period of time. There are examples from some of these projects scattered throughout the book to illustrate the basic principles put forward. What follows is a very brief description of the main projects referred to which should help in the general understanding of the text.

The battery-separator project consisted of making thick pads of absorbent material in ultra-thin glass wool and cellulose to retain the electrolyte (sulphuric acid) inside battery accumulators. The product features a better resistance to acid than pure cellulose. It raises battery performance levels and reduces electrolyte consumption, so maintenance is easier.

The filtration membrane project consisted of making tubular membranes to be used in ultra-fine filtration for the food industry, the pharmaceutical industry, waste water treatment, etc. One of the filter's features is that it can be unclogged, disinfected and sterilized by a reverse steam flow due to its exceptionally high mechanical, chemical and thermal resistance levels.

The heat transfer fluid project developed a synthetic thermal fluid with high-level heat characteristics. It can operate at high temperatures and avoids using steam networks that are costly and dangerous, because they work at very high pressures. The new fluid has much better temperature resistance than competing mineral oils that deteriorate rapidly with heat. At the other end of the spectrum, it stays liquid well below 0°C, which means it's now conceivable to have thermodynamic loops that carry both high and low temperatures.

The non-destructive laser control project consisted of creating ultrasonic waves inside an object by means of laser impulses. The laser induces rapid, alternating, localized stress cycles that generate ultrasonic waves. Outgoing ultrasonic waves are then compared to ingoing waves. This makes it possible to detect flaws that are invisible to the naked eye. The process is based on the same principles as classic ultrasonic echography but it has the enormous competitive advantage of not necessitating contact, whether the waves are ingoing or outgoing. This means you can detect flaws in moving parts, or in parts situated in areas that are inaccessible to bulkier conventional instruments with their gauges, transmission gel, cables, etc.

In the composite material project they developed a manufacturing process for carbon fibre parts that could reproduce the parts in strict conformity. This material was essentially construed for the sports and leisure industries.

The project on reinforcement fibre for concrete developed a

supple metal fibre that's tough and rustproof. When you mix it with concrete you get very high mechanical resistance levels, you do away with conventional techniques like rods or netting and your concrete lasts longer. The references made to this project concern the very early development phases (1984) and don't give a promising picture. But today the company has overcome most of its difficulties and the fibre is now commercialized.

The measurement (or instrument control) computer project developed a dedicated machine to monitor measurement bays. Whenever needed, this computer triggers off or stops instruments that measure or control industrial processes or experiments.

In the project for a machine to make electronic substrate they developed new equipment to produce semiconductor plates (or wafers) for use in the manufacture of integrated circuits and electronic components. The process used is called CVD (chemical vapour deposition). It consists of sublimating a solid source (in powder form) at high temperature, then conveying it on a flow of inert gas as far as a plate, where it forms a semiconducting crystalline deposit. This way, you get thin crystalline layers with a diameter of about 100 to 200 mm. There's less scrap, so the machine brings significant gains in productivity and output once the process has been optimized and all related production technology (heat control, fluid distribution, modelling) fully integrated. The equipment is also safer to use and more environmentally friendly because it does away with using toxic gases (metal chlorides in particular).

The special optical fibre project developed optical fibre that could transmit very low frequency light waves with low attenuation levels.

The high-speed machining project consisted of developing new principles, machines and tools to cut metal about ten to twenty times faster. To give an example, that means a transition from cutting speeds of 30 m/mn to cutting speeds of 600 m/mn. The main effect is a drastic reduction in machining time. It's a particularly valuable asset with very big parts like ship engines, where it usually takes 24 hours to machine the upper side of the crankcase.

Elf-Atochem developed a material called "breathable". It's

watertight, but permeable to air. This permeability is also selective, which is a definite advantage with fruit and vegetable packing. The fresh produce is able to "breathe" and the exchange of air with the environment plays a vital role in preserving foods of this kind. Appropriate packing thus considerably prolongs shelf-life.

It's because this book is based on practical experience that it has a particular message. A particular message for innovators who are fed up with hearing that when good companies launch good products on a good market they have better chances of succeeding than poor companies who launch poor products on poor markets.

A particular message for project leaders who are disappointed by a large number of methods of analysis that say "This is where you stand", and then leave you to muddle through. And a particular message for those who have come to realize that products don't necessarily have the right qualities just because they're flawless. The fact is that people don't buy products for the defects they don't have. They buy them for the qualities they do have.

This book could also be of help to students doing commercial studies or engineering studies who are keen to increase their knowledge of marketing in industry before they start their careers in that sector. Whichever the case may be, this book is an attempt to encourage non-fatalistic, independent attitudes. It's there to say and to make people say:

- Yes, I can get the competitive advantage instead of trailing behind.
- Yes, I can get a hold on the market and swing it in my favour instead of always trying to adapt to it.
- Yes, I can make customers want to come and buy my products instead of always having to bow to customer requirements.
- Yes, I can reverse the balance of power and influence this environment instead of having the environment run my life.

In this critical period, more and more analyses encourage enterpreneurship (Fauconnier, 1996). This book brings some basic, down-to-earth rules that will give you systematic and constructive guidance in launching a new business. And since we don't always inherit the most ideal situations to start off with, it shows us the way to take things in hand and draw maximum profit from the capital we already possess in technology. As the proverb says, "God helps those who help themselves". Or, to put it in the more philosophical terms of Bachelard (1983), "Nothing can be taken for granted, nothing is given, everything is constructed".

REFERENCES

Bachelard, G. (1983). *La formation de l'esprit scientifique*, 12th edition. Paris: Librairie Philosophique J. Vrin.

Buzzel, R.D. and Gale, B.T. (1987). *The PIMS. Principles Linking Strategy to Performance*. New York: The Free Press.

Callon, M. (ed.) (1989). L'agonie d'un laboratoire. In *La science et ses réseaux*. Paris: La Découverte.

Clugston, C.O. (1995). High-tech demands own new-product plan. *Electronic News*, 4 December.

Fauconnier, P. (1996). *Le talent qui dort, La France en panne d'entrepreneurs*. Paris: Editions du Seuil, Collection "L'histoire immédiate".

Peters, T. and Waterman, R. (1982). *In Search of Excellence*. New York: Harper Business.

1
Marketing Technological Innovations

ILL-ADAPTED THEORIES

A Very High Infant Mortality Rate

Some worrying figures have been published on innovation. About 70% of the attempts to launch products are estimated to fail (Booz, Allen & Hamilton, 1971; Mansfield and Wagner, 1975; Clugston, 1995). And out of all the industrial products successfully developed from a technological viewpoint, fewer than 50% achieve commercial success (Choffray and Dorey, 1983). But then, what do we mean exactly by failure and by innovation?

Generally speaking, you can consider that product launching has failed in the following three cases:

1 When the product never in fact goes on the market, although the company has invested in Research and Development.
2 When the product is taken off the market shortly after being launched because it doesn't sell, in spite of the company's efforts.
3 When the company is constantly injecting money to prolong the life of the product artificially because it can't survive alone: in other words, it isn't profitable.

It seems harder to define innovation clearly. First, "innovation" is synonymous with "new product", so you can't define one by the other. Books on the subject describe different types of innovation, then classify them according to how new the innovations actually are. For instance, there are repositioned products (because customer attitude has changed), products with new compositions (where the physical characteristics have been modified) or original products (breakthrough innovations).

But definitions of "innovation" or "new product" in the broad sense are few and far between, almost as if new products were new products just because they were different from what they were before. The most you can say is that innovation is "a new combination of existing elements of knowledge in the form of devices that are potentially useful to the economy" (Silem, 1991), or again, that "innovation is the transforming, by real-life application, of theoretical inventions or discoveries that reveal what already exists but was not yet known" (Grawitz, 1986).

If we want to see our way clearly round the book, we first need to get orientated among all these sweeping generalities. Then the next step will be to set limits by restricting our field to innovative products or innovative services in industry. This means we shall only be talking about products or services for sale or rent to companies or, more generally speaking, to organizations, that is, industrial marketing, as opposed to consumer marketing which consists of selling products to consumers. Basically, what characterizes industrial marketing is the fact that it deals with group purchasing, where customers exert a direct influence on suppliers. And the fewer customers there are, the more influential each one is going to be.

We will then go on to differentiate between innovative industrial products by comparing where they originate. The first innovations stem from customer observations, when customers give suppliers ideas for potential products. More often than not these new ideas express real problems that clients are addressing, so the results are eagerly awaited when suppliers actually do meet customer expectations. This kind of innovation is often said to be incremental because it marginally improves the product but is still based on something customers know and can refer to. Chapelet and Mangione (1995), for instance, give ideas on new product launching that you can apply here. Well-tried principles like theirs all reduce to adapting your marketing techniques to the pre-launch period. Basically, the specificity of this approach lies in the fact that you set up a file on marketing for the first time. And setting up this initial basis for reflection on marketing requires a special effort, both qualitatively and quantitatively.

On the other hand, the second category of innovations is developed at the suppliers' initiative. They're the ones who had the ideas and came up with the new designs or who had the idea of applying particular technology to areas that weren't originally targeted. For instance, a company that's developed a pressure gauge for aeronautics might try to apply it to the chemical industry. This type of innovation is often called breakthrough innovation. The product isn't solicited by customers here, as it is with first-category innovations. You could even say it's a nuisance to them. They're forced to change their usual ways of purchasing, working with design, carrying out maintenance. In fact, their work routine as a whole.

This book was conceived to address the second category of innovations in particular. It's an area that marketing has so far tended to ignore, but it fully deserves our attention according to Foster (1986) because even if it only represents 20% of all innovations these 20% have a far greater market impact. For convenience we shall refer to them as technological innovations or technologically innovative products and consider them to be based on new technology or on technology that's sufficiently different from existing techniques to disrupt customer work and purchasing routines. One example here would be a new composite material introduced as a substitute for metal. Buyers wouldn't know on which criteria to base their opinion. They would also have to learn how to implement the new material and ensure its correct maintenance.

This initial definition, made from a marketing standpoint, seems to imply that the technological innovation concept has more to do with customers than with the state of technology at a given time. Taking this to extremes you could say that an electric vacuum cleaner sold to bushmen in a remote area would be a technological innovation. Identical products can in fact mean something entirely different from one country to another. For example, 3M's kitchen scouring pads are a huge success in Pakistan and Egypt, although they have to be sold in much smaller sizes than the format we're familiar with. They come in detachable squares the size of postage stamps to make the price more accessible. A luxury product that's in direct competition with sand. In other words, from a marketing outlook, the product's position on the market outweighs the product itself.

On the other hand, a digital telephone, with more complex and more recent technology than an analogue telephone, wouldn't be considered technologically innovative if this didn't change anything for the user. It would be a different case, though, if the telephone provided access to other consumer-friendly services such as teleconferencing, automatic recall or call transfer. One of the characteristics of technological innovations is that they're even harder to put on the market than the others, with failure rates of 95% recorded.

Market Turbulence

Let's try to classify the situation a little. All the different cases of technological innovation studied have one feature in common: turbulence. And this turbulence usually begins when the product's technological development gets underway. Technological development actually modifies market dynamics by updating the market or by outdating it. It can transform the shape and structure of markets by extending them and modifying their segmentation. It can likewise change the face of competition by bringing in new competitors from unexpected areas. A good illustration of this type of upheaval is the watch industry, which grew, underwent restructuring and then met with new competition when quartz movements suddenly took over from mechanical ones (Figure 1.1)

Turbulence has several possible sources, as shown in Figure 1.2. Imagine you're located in the centre of the diagram. If your technology evolves it may set up a ripple effect and put your customers' or your competitors' technological choices in doubt. Your customers' technology is downstream. It may evolve to such an extent that you have to carry out more research yourself. For example, your customer switches from a "copper" support to an "optical fibre" support to transmit measurements. Accordingly, you will have to develop a new range of products to take

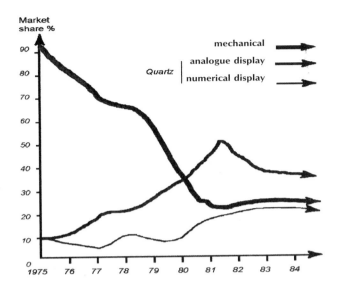

Figure 1.1 *Technological turbulence in the watch industry.*
Source: *Rapport sur l'état de la technique.* Science et Technicians, *Special Issue, March 1995,*
p. 12

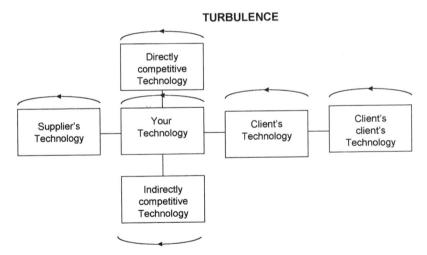

Figure 1.2 *Technological environment of the innovation (inspired by Porter)*

the measurements you don't yet know how to take with optical
fibre (e.g. reflectometrics). A technical change by the customer is
bound to disrupt your work too. Your suppliers' technology may
evolve too, upstream, forcing you to make new choices or take
up new challenges in technology.

Similarly, the advent of digital controls has revolutionized the machine-tool industry by obliging constructors to automate and use electronics. It has also revolutionized customer perception of machines. They have the impression they're buying digital control systems nowadays, not machine tools.

Figure 1.2 has another dimension to it, and this is competition-related. There are two possible types of competition in technology:

- Direct competitive technology competes directly with you over a core product. With reinforced concrete, for example, a reinforcing fibre would be directly competitive technology for traditional reinforcement.
- Indirect competitive technology occurs when one technology prevents another from developing, but isn't a substitute for it. The freezing of liquids is not a form of packing but it would jeopardize bottle sales all the same. Likewise, disposable garments and washing machines to remove dirt ultrasonically would be technologies that compete indirectly with detergent. They would harm detergent sales without actually being washing agents themselves.

Generally speaking, you can say that turbulence in technology creates great uncertainty. We shall call this technological uncertainty. It gives innovators the impression that their markets lack transparency. They don't know where to go, how to go there or what to offer because the information they normally use for decision making doesn't exist or doesn't exist any more. Either there's no past or it's vanished. This turbulence is also visible at the customer level. Decisions must be made without a reference system because everything clients are familiar with has changed.

To sum up, marketers of technologically innovative industrial products may meet with the following situations:

- Breakthrough situations when technological innovations emerge from research and markets are not the same before and after their release. This is partly due to the impact.
- Marketing situations where research is involved. Either research is involved at the researchers' own initiative or it has been brought in to restore a balance because of outside turbulence in technology.

- Situations where technological innovations disrupt customers' regular buying habits and work routine. As the customers' reference system is no longer valid, they can't evaluate the offer being made to them. On top of this, they must learn to work differently.
- Situations where innovation causes major changes to the rules of competition within a given industry.

With the breakthroughs we shall be looking at, market dynamics change and no longer conform to the same rules. Frontiers either open out or close in. Innovation of this kind modifies the rules of competition, updates some parts of industry and makes some others obsolete.

Customers react differently with breakthroughs because this type of innovation provides another choice, they have no criteria to screen it and they don't know how to weigh up their requirements correctly in relation to it. In fact, industrial clients' reactions may seem irrational in situations like this, even paradoxical, compared to usual. They're completely in the dark, but they may say "yes", which entirely contradicts what industrial marketing usually teaches you.

Breakthroughs that arise out of research programmes often transform the usual customer approach to buying or working. Latour (1989) cites the example of Kodak, who "invented the amateur photography market" when they took on film development. The only prior market was that of the professional photographers who developed their own photographs. In fact, whenever breakthroughs emerge from research you can say the markets were non-existent beforehand quite simply because the innovations created them.

Even in cases where markets existed prior to breakthroughs, innovations can modify market structure. Take the watch market, for instance. It underwent changes through the introduction of quartz, although it existed long before quartz appeared.

How Can Competition Alter the Face of the Market?

The Analograph company had been manufacturing graphic recorders[1] for many years and they knew their products and their markets well. These were split up into three segments: process control, fine-tuning of laboratory prototypes and maintenance diagnosis. But the graphic recorder industry was set back by the sudden appearance of computers, which did the same job and more. The arrival of this new technology on the traditional market was enough to change its structure entirely. Not all customers had the same attitude to computers, which meant they no longer had the same attitude to graphic recorders. So Analograph had to transform their segmentation by going from three to nine segments, as illustrated in Figure 1.3.

In this particular case they went to see Research and asked "What offers can we come up with if we want to compete as long as possible in satisfactory financial conditions, with new competition like this and market trends going the way they are?"

If you look back at all the cases described above you can sum up by saying that market turbulence always has similar implications for innovators. Give or take a few variations, they have to:

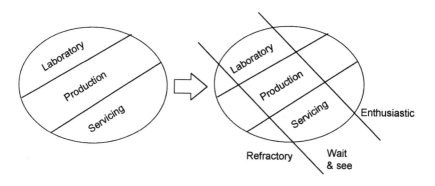

Figure 1.3 *Segmentation changes due to arrival of the innovation*

---

[1] Graphic recorders are instruments which measure variations in physical characteristics (e.g. temperature) in relation to time and record them on paper unrolling at constant speed.

- Define or redefine their field of activity
- Segment or re-segment their market
- Develop or modify their market
- Evaluate or re-evaluate very changeable and varied competition, and position or reposition themselves in relation to that challenge
- Understand the way customers react today.

Inadequate Models

Research and Development play an important role in the preceding descriptions, first, on a very basic level, in product conception and development and then, at a less obvious level, in marketing. In fact it's often too late to correct imperfections by the time the products go on the market. There's no going back. Either products live up to customer expectations, in which case the chances are they will be diffused, or they're badly designed and unlikely to sell.

This critical situation originates in the sequence order of the innovation's development process (i.e. first, the idea is put out, then screened, next the concept is developed, then the product designed, introduced on the market, diffused). Perhaps this linear concept of the development process and product diffusion is instructive, but it doesn't give a good enough explanation of how things really happen.

If you want to fathom the cause of these inadequacies you must take a good look at the product life-cycle model. This is frequently used in marketing today. It began with the diffusion theory, on which Rogers (1976) has inventoried literally thousands of studies in various disciplines. Product life-cycle has played an altogether predominant role in innovation management and is often given as a universal model that's applicable to any products. The most typical version of it is shown in Figure 1.4.

You can predict product diffusion with this model as soon as you have your first sales figures. It's said to be deterministic because everything in it happens as if the product's future life was determined by the first few months. The claim is that it automatically indicates what to do during each phase of the cycle

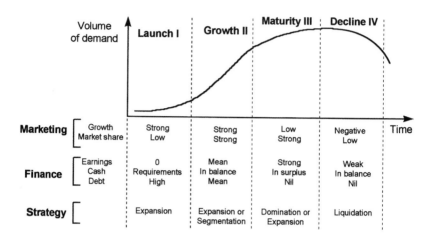

Figure 1.4   *Normative product life-cycle model (adapted from Martinet, 1983)*

(e.g. domination, liquidation). And thanks to this potential it's understood to be normative, because it provides norms to act on.

However, there may be some doubt as to the validity of this theory if you're dealing with technological innovations. The fact is that you forget one essential thing when you take this model to be universal. It's only adapted to products that have passed the launch phase. And if you refer back to those failure rate figures of 95%, then in theory the curve for 95% of these technological innovations is generally as shown in Figure 1.5.

In spite of appearances, this figure doesn't put the validity of the product life-cycle model in doubt. It simply criticizes the application of the model to technological innovations that haven't begun their launch phase and rejects the idea that the model is inherently deterministic. Even if the figures given previously are inaccurate, it's clear that the mere fact of putting a product on the market doesn't mean it will achieve regular and lasting diffusion in line with the S-shaped curve.

So what makes us think that we can reject this model as far as technological innovations are concerned? Simply this: the initial conditions necessary for applying the model are not all there. As we said, the product life-cycle model is normative in the sense that it indicates what to do at each phase. But it has to be deterministic before it can be normative: that is, if you know one point on the curve, that's enough for you to be able to forecast

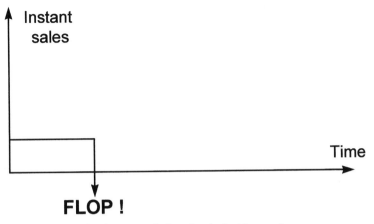

Figure 1.5   *"Life-cycle" for 95% of all technological innovations*

the way things are evolving. Not only this. In order to be deterministic, the model has to be probabilistic and statistical (using given predictions, together with their probabilities) and it must be the result of a large number of observations. When you build a model like this, you're implicitly supposed to think that what you're looking at results from the cumulative evolution of many different variables, agents and events, and that each one of these has a very slight influence on the whole. The model is said to conform to the law of numbers.

But this doesn't apply when you're putting an industrial product on the market for the first time. On the contrary, you're in a different situation here with only a few agents on the market. Yet each of them can wield sufficient weight to determine the product's future.

Imagine the Channel Tunnel is built with fibre concrete (i.e. concrete reinforced with fibre that has high mechanical resistance levels). If it comes off, this experiment will give fibre concrete the initial boost needed to launch it on the construction market. On the other hand, if the tunnel collapses during inauguration and carries off the Minister of Transport and all the local dignitaries with it, publicity will be devastating and a lot of costly effort will go to ruin. One specific event when a market is just getting underway can be enough to set a project on the path to success or failure.

Besides, if you consider that diffusion models are partly based on imitation, with diffusion speeds calculated on what proportion of the population has been reached so far and what proportion hasn't, then you can justifiably say that conditions for using these methods are limit here in the mathematical sense. They're limit because the population reached so far is nil and the population that remains to be reached is indeterminate and subject to change.

Not one study on the Mansfield type model (1961) or the Blackmann type model (1974) has ever measured the amount of error induced in diffusion curves by the underlying hypothesis signifying that "innovators"[2] have already adopted the product or process by time $t = 0$ (Figure 1.6). And actually, to be quite honest, our real problem is understanding why innovators adopt the product or the process in the first place.

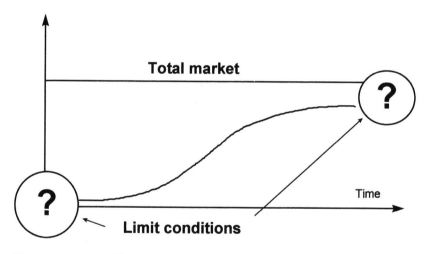

Figure 1.6   *Using diffusion curves in limit conditions*

Success and Failure Factors: "Mountains that Bring Forth Mice"

All these unsuccessful attempts to launch new products have caught the attention of numerous writers, and books abound

---

[2]   "Innovators" has the same sense here as it has in the diffusion theory, where 2.5% of the innovators between -3σ and -2σ on the Gauss curve are called innovators.

where authors try to pin down success and failure factors. In most cases these studies are based on observations from a large number of projects. Quantities of data have been collected on many "scientifically" processed variables. There's unquestionably been a lot of work done on the subject, but what's the real outcome of it? A bibliographical summary of this literature (Millier, 1993) helps to list factors that give the most frequent or most convincing explanations for success or failure with new products.

The following success factors can be inventoried:

1 At product or technology level:
   - New products are unique or higher quality than competitor products
   - Meet customer needs
   - Fit firm's production skills and resources
   - Fit into firm's production lines
   - Fit firm's engineering skills and resources.
2 At market level:
   - The new product market is large and rapidly growing
   - Has few competitors
   - Has demand
   - Has a concentrated market (i.e. a few big customers: 20–80 as a rule).
3. At company level:
   - The company has high-level proficiency and experience; is proactive in market need identification
   - Has well-targeted marketing (advertising, promotion, sales force)
   - Has good knowledge of market (preliminary evaluation)
   - Has efficient launch procedure (timely actions, incremental development with each phase controlled)
   - Is interactive with customers (testing and implication)
   - Maintains sales effort after launch (no flash-in-the-pan products)
   - Has marketing and development interaction (good company climate)
   - Has technical competence
   - Has legal coverage (patents)
   - Has experienced project manager (enthusiastic, involved, with status, responsibility)

658.8 MIL
ACC. NO   19802
Limerick Institute of Technology - LIBRARY
Institiúid Teicneolaíochta Luimnigh - LEABHARLANN

- Has well-defined aims (project end-use)
- Has support and involvement from general management
- Has help from outside specialists.

Non-influential factors on success or failure are as follows:

- Company characteristics (sector, turnover, nationality)
- Total R&D expenditure
- Project type (push or pull)
- Technical complexity
- Quality of production start-up
- First or second ranking on market
- A sole competitor.

Failure factors given are:

1 At product or technology level:
   - The new product employs leading-edge technology unfamiliar to firm
   - Doesn't fit into firm's existing product lines
   - Is little better than competitor products
   - Is not technically viable (deficient product)
   - Is too highly priced (or makes no obvious savings for customer).
2 At market level:
   - There is frequent introduction of new products
   - Customer satisfaction with existing offer
   - Strong, well-established competition.
3 At company level:
   - The company shows poor evaluation of market needs
   - Poor quantitative evaluation of market
   - Inefficient marketing (ill-adapted marketing effort)
   - Insufficient investment in sales and marketing organizations
   - Deficient after-sales service
   - Lack of communication
   - Neglect of environmental problems (norms, regulations)
   - Lack of legal protection (patents)
   - Poor control of product development
   - Real development costs above forecast
   - R&D/Marketing interface problems (dysfunction, disagreement)
   - Lack of organizational flexibility.

You don't have to be an expert to see that this mountain of work will only "bring forth a mouse" in terms of results. Anybody will tell you that you have better chances of succeeding if your product is good and your company is rich and competent with big, non-competitive markets, than if your product is poor and your company poor and incompetent with shrinking markets and raging competition!

Marketers encounter two basic problems when they want to use this literature in day-to-day innovation management. First, there are numerous criteria listed and these are in the form of a checklist of the conditions you need to meet before proceeding with the launch. This can give you the impression that everything's important and that you will have to tackle it all. On the contrary, I've often learnt from personal experience that you can succeed without having all these factors at the same time. But you must choose your key success factors after very keen analysis, carefully and with respect to the situation. Another point is that having a few very strong key factors can promote work ties and thus improve other elements. It all comes down to saying you should build on your strong points and according to your capacities. You don't need the same qualities to succeed as a variety artist, a priest, an accountant or a managing director.

When they collected these criteria the authors did a statistician's or an academic's job and compiled a sort of dictionary of essential success factors. But unfortunately nobody can speak a foreign language with just a dictionary and the uninitiated will find their information hard to apply, because the indispensable grammar book is missing. Hard to apply because nobody really knows how to make a good product, how to be competent, how to find receptive markets and how to go about bringing these success factors together.

Furthermore, the authors always proceeded in the same way by studying projects *after* their success or failure, which meant they only looked at results, not at processes. So their observations fail to address real management problems in the sense that They're retrospective and have little relevance for managers who need to act here and now. If you're still not convinced of the inadequacy of this type of approach, take a look at the Diesel case reported in Callon and Latour (1985).

To cut a long story short in the late nineteenth century Rudolf

Diesel invented an internal combustion engine, patented it, built a prototype, had it manufactured and sold it to his first customers with a satisfaction-or-your-money-back guarantee. But, and here's the crunch, the engine turned out to be unreliable, fragile, costly, oversized and particularly useless. The fact is that customers were using steam then to drive their high-power engines and they were perfectly satisfied. The daring few who bought the engine were soon disappointed and demanded a refund. And Diesel went bankrupt and committed suicide.

You only need to apply the success factor/failure factor approach to the Diesel case to see that:

- The engine was little better than its competitor (the steam engine)
- The engine was technically deficient
- The engine didn't save the customers any money
- The engine didn't correspond to market needs
- Diesel wasn't familiar with the market
- Diesel wasn't familiar with his customers' requirements
- Diesel took the wrong approach to launching.

In short, failure was inevitable, almost as if there were some divine justice which decreed that those who lived in error would die by error too.

But this argument no longer applies today when you realize that the vast majority of trucks, large electric power generators, ships, locomotives and about half the new cars sold in France have diesel-powered engines. So here we are with a situation the theory doesn't account for, where an inventor who's neither rich nor competent nor well informed sells a poor product that ends up by imposing itself! There's still hope, then, of improving on the explanations given *after the events* by these books.

The only way to really understand why a project either hurtles to its doom or soars towards success is to keep up a close analysis of how the project proceeds, from the start right up to product launch. This means observing the process while it's underway so that you can see what happens, rather than noting results and trying to imagine what led to them.

Callon and Latour (1985) take up the story of Diesel's engine again to tell how army representatives suddenly became interested in it after the inventor died in 1913. They were looking for a compact, powerful, self-driven source of mechanical energy to put in the submarines they planned to develop in case world war broke out. Henceforth, hundreds of man-years were devoted to the engine's development, with a particular focus on the submarine application. Then, and only then, did the engine become sturdy, economical, reliable, compact, useful and attractive. In short, a good product.

We shall adopt this principle of process observation and attempt to find another explanation for so many abortive innovations (Millier, 1987). An illustration of this approach would be to say that it's easier to understand the circumstances of an accident from a film than from a newspaper photo.

From what we've seen here, observing the actual project process provides some hope of improving on simple explanations for success or failure. It's even conceivable to discover some action sequences that would give you winning strategies for innovation projects. As we said previously, a product begins life well before it's put on the market just as a child begins well before birth. If you pursue this comparison, it means in theory that you can start to apply marketing to your product at the research stage, the way you start supervising and caring for a baby during pregnancy. Industrial products have another life, so to speak, prior to their actual life-cycle.

THE LIFE-CYCLE OF TECHNOLOGICAL INNOVATIONS AND THE TRANSITORY STATE

The Life-cycle of a Technological Innovation Project

It seems clear that we need to worry about what happens before the product goes on the market, so we can now use the "project life-cycle" concept to give some sort of tangibility to the product's gestation period. This concept is used to visualize all the activities a company develops around a product before launching it. We shall make an analogy with product life-cycle by representing project life with an S-curve. To begin with (Booz, Allen & Hamilton, 1971) , we'll link these two cycles in a project–product continuum as shown in Figure 1.7.

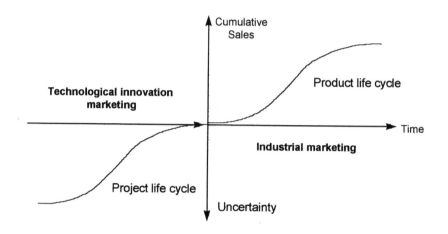

Figure 1.7   *Project–product continuum*

Cycle Discontinuity

You realize, though, when you see what really happens, that product management modes are very different before and after launching and that a hypothetical project–product continuum is hardly feasible. The fact is that during the R&D phases the products are run by research laboratories or by development teams that have their own objectives, rules and constraints. Their objective could be, for instance, to make a technically viable product. And they will only have an expense budget — that's considered to be an investment.

But the marketing and sales functions have an entirely different set of objectives, rules and constraints once the products are on the market. Marketing goals may be product growth or diffusion and the budget will have to balance out expenditure and income within the framework of a profit and loss account. These few indications go to show that there's a world of difference between project management and product management. This discontinuity can be visualized as in Figure 1.8.

Yet closer empirical observation reveals that there's still more to it than discontinuity. When you talk to industrial marketers about their projects you realize that this discontinuity has both

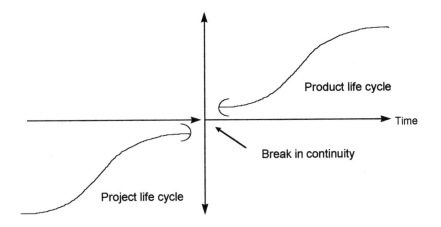

Figure 1.8 *Continuity break in project–product development process*

substance and duration. What examples do they give us?

- "The army ordered 150 items from us before the product had been advertised and published in the catalogue. It was our marketing function that sold them, not our salesmen."
- "The products don't follow the traditional product life-cycle curve after launching." There are phases like stairs that give the following shape to the curve shown in Figure 1.9.

The first phase can be explained by eager innovators and competitors rushing to get hold of the product. It's more a

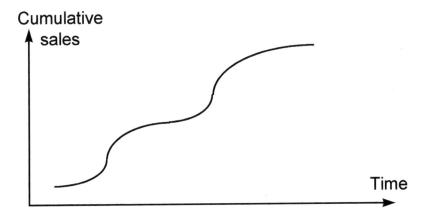

Figure 1.9 *Stair-pattern diffusion curve*

question of customers coming to buy the product than suppliers selling it to them. The salesmen only really come on the scene during the second phase when information is available about customer use and product utility. With the help of this data, salesmen can wield suitable arguments and back them up too.

- "We sell 700 tons a year of our product to Japan, but our customers don't want to tell us what they do with it."
- "We sold 15 tons all in one go to a customer for tests but we don't know what kind of tests and we don't know when we'll get another order like it."
- "We were selling our gas to prolong shelf-life but in fact our customers were buying it to set off their high-range products."
- "Nobody has ever earned anything in robotics. It's as if robotics never reached the maturity stage and the innovation just didn't create a monopoly in the innovators' favour."

The same question underlies all these remarks, and that is: When does the product life-cycle actually begin? There are sales recorded in the examples given, but they don't go through the usual company channels. Or then, again, customers intend to use the product for something suppliers don't know, don't understand and can't promote it for. This all comes down to saying that what customers buy is different from what suppliers sell them. Product definition is always mobile. It changes from day to day as customers learn to understand the product better and suppliers acquire a better understanding of what their customers are buying from them. The following is an example to illustrate the fact that a product's definition can change even when its composition, functionality and shape remain the same.

A company had developed a steam-compression evaporator which was used to evaporate water, as its name indicates. Well, half of the customers failed to grasp what the evaporator could do for them until it was presented as a solid waste extractor. In fact the important thing for them was to recover dry or concentrated matter rather than to get rid of water. What they valued was the solid waste, whereas the others valued the water.

Existence of a Transitory State

These situations are typical of periods of turbulence. But which part of the cycle should you link with the turbulence phase? Project life or product life? All these inconsistencies between the facts and the model mean that you will have to develop the model even further by stretching the boundaries of discontinuity. You can represent product–project life in three quite distinct phases if you do this (Millier, 1989).

- *Research project life-cycle.* This represents what happens during project conception and feasibility phases. We shall say that this phase corresponds to a permanent system state, meaning here that the project is run entirely from a research point of view in conformance with well-established logic and rules.
- *Product life-cycle.* This represents product sales evolution after the product has been launched on the market. This phase has the characteristics of a permanent system as well. The product is run uniquely from a marketing standpoint, with set rules and logic.
- *Technological innovation life-cycle.* This is situated between the first two cycles and represents the entire phase of project derivation. It is where the product changes from a laboratory device into a desirable product. We shall make an analogy with physical, electrical or mechanical phenomena and call this intermediate state by the convenient name of "transitory state". In contrast, there are permanent system states on either side of it, with rules of evolution that you can model.

As from here we can represent the project–product evolution process as in Figure 1.10. We won't link the transitory state (representing technological innovation) to project life-cycle or to product life-cycle because of the problems we brought up earlier, but will consider this phase to be in a category of its own within the project life.

If you accept these principles and also the fact that marketing deals mainly with products already on the market, then you can consider that marketing technologically innovative industrial products covers the entire pre-launch period, as shown in Figure 1.10. You will then be able to position this type of marketing in a product evolution/time perspective.

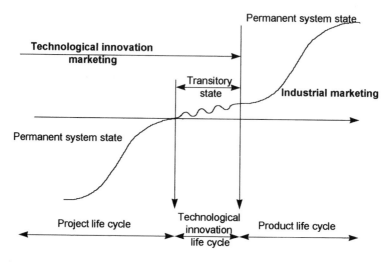

Figure 1.10   *Transitory phase in the project–product continuum*

THE FIELD OF APPLICATION FOR TECHNOLOGICAL INNOVATION MARKETING

Now we have situated innovative product marketing, we shall go over the types of product it most applies to and deduce from this which products are unlikely to be applicable. First, technologically innovative products are bound to incur changes in users' work routines. This distinction automatically bars projects relating to me-too type products or repositioned products. For example, launching a copy of the IBM-PC wouldn't be technological innovation marketing. It would be a classical approach, typical of new product launching (see, for example, Choffray and Dorey, 1983, or Chapelet and Mangione, 1995). The key driving force behind it would be aggressive marketing tactics like promotion, unbeatable prices, distribution.

We have also seen that technologically innovative industrial products both cause and experience turbulence, and the uncertainty that breeds. There again, this precludes all projects (even ones with highly complex technology) that develop in a reassuring climate, because these innovators know where they're going. The market isn't uncertain: their technology won't create turbulence for the company. A new type of nuclear power plant in France, for instance, wouldn't be a part of the technologically innovative market because its market is clearly situated and there's only one customer. Ariane rockets or military projects, which are developed to specifications with orderbook guarantees, are out, too. You're dealing with complex project organization and project marketing here.

First and foremost, an industrial product with innovative technology is an industrial product. That means you can leave aside all projects that develop products for the general public, even if they're sufficiently innovative to create markets. In fact, these projects target consumer marketing where customers are numerous, lack technical expertise and can't define their needs in technical terms. For example, camcorders or compact discs aren't applicable here, however educational they might be, because they're developed from start to finish by the same manufacturers and because they need to work faultlessly for consumers right from the word go.

To sum up, technologically innovative industrial product marketing relates to:

- Industrial product development projects that disrupt customers' work routine and purchasing habits
- Projects faced with turbulence problems (in technology or sales), which create uncertainty and opacity
- All projects involving R&D work, whatever the size of the company and even if it's just being set up
- Projects in a transitory state between R&D and commercialization.

On the other hand, the following projects don't concern us:

- Projects for consumer product development
- Projects concerning me-too or repositioned products
- Projects developing products for calm or predetermined markets (big space programmes, for example).

Note: The term "product" as used in the above paragraph is to be taken in the broad sense, meaning product or service. You can in fact apply the same rules to industrial services or to industrial products, provided they answer to the characteristics listed above (i.e. disruption, uncertainty, turbulence, R&D involvement). Both technologically innovative services and products are rather intangible, which means customers never know beforehand what they're buying.

What future profits can an adult education business guarantee a company director who enrols staff for a seminar on neurolinguistic programming? What returns on investment can customers be sure of getting if they buy a server and Internet access from a provider? In both these cases, purchase decisions will be made without any real guarantees, but suppliers have to convince their customers to buy all the same.

Integrating International Perspectives

In most cases, the only viable markets for technological innovations (the ones studied in this book, in particular) are either European or global. So the markets we refer to are international for the most part. However, as technological innovation is quite radical by definition, the international aspect is taken to be just one more element in the diversity of each case we look at. There won't be any specific differentiation of international cases as a group.

It can be easier and more feasible to pick segments in your own country. On the other hand, it's quite possible for English, French, German and Swedish laboratories to encounter the same problems and share the same enthusiasm over a new surface-analyser using particle bombardment, for example. In fact, it's more logical to have a broadly international approach to segmentation here. All the research laboratories will be grouped in the same segment and served the same way.

As with other aspects of the book, what we attempt to do is to keep the international aspect as specific as possible to technological innovation. This implies that we won't be discussing commonplaces that are equally relevant to ordinary products. Risk coverage on exports, for example. The fact that it doesn't pay to have ethnic differences between vendors and customers. Or the fact that it costs more to work abroad than at home.

It should be stressed, however, that local competitors very often have a major advantage over foreign suppliers. The risk might be that some German clients, for instance, should contact their regular domestic suppliers and say "We have just been contacted by a foreign competitor of yours who showed us a very interesting new concept in non-destructive control. Couldn't you offer us something equivalent?"

It certainly isn't unusual to find a marked difference in behaviour between European customers. According to Roland Calori (1991):

- German consumers are chauvinistic and cold. Germany is the country of differentiation and regionalization.
- British consumers are price-sensitive and take profit. Great Britain is the champion of liberalism.
- Dutch consumers are thrifty and critical. The Netherlands is the champion of internationalization.
- Spanish consumers are extremist. Spain is regionalized with regional leaders.
- French consumers are impulsive and like novelty. France has strong competition at the European level and is a country of strong state intervention.
- Italian consumers are impulsive and take care of their look. Italy is a dual country. North and South. Modern companies and archaic ones.
- Scandinavian consumers are quality-minded and critical ... even more than the Dutch. Denmark has high taxes.

But you seldom come across such detail. The general tendency is to distinguish between Northern countries, Anglo-Saxon countries (Germany, Great Britain), Southern Europe (Spain, Italy) and East European countries.

Finally, it seems clear that the construction of Europe and the pressure of international competition is more than likely to affect industrialists' attitudes in time to come. As Frank Bradley (1991) says: "Recognizing that a key strength of the United States and Japan is a large uniform domestic market, European businesses are beginning to discard the antiquated idea that prosperity derives from protected markets."

Checklist

- Innovations fail to penetrate in 70% of the cases. A lot has been written to try to explain why with the help of the crucial success factor/crucial failure factor approach. But this method isn't very helpful to project managers because it's an *after* attempt to link up the characteristics of product situation with end results. It doesn't analyse the project as it goes along. In fact it's a rigid approach to an accomplished fact; it only tells you where you are but not what you should do. So much the better if you've managed to reunite the necessary success factors. If not, too bad! This is why the success/failure factor approach fails to elucidate when or why a project ultimately prospers or doesn't. It's also true to say that the factors which are supposed to explain success or failure are commonplaces. They more or less amount to saying that a good product launched by a good company on a good market has better chances of succeeding than a bad one from a poor company on a poor market.

- The product life-cycle model is often used in marketing. But it isn't well adapted to technical innovation because it implies having sales data on the initial months, whereas in fact the initial months of a technical innovation are well upstream to launching. However, you can't wait for the product to go on the market before you start marketing it. So technical innovation marketing will be considered as a sort of introduction of the project to its potential environ-ment and we shall describe this pre-launch period as the innovation project life-cycle.

- There's a phase called the "transitory phase" during the innovation's project life-cycle. It's situated between research and product launching. The project is still run by the company's technical department here, even though market-ing is already involved. During this period, suppliers invest by carrying out full-scale experiments with customers to develop the product. But they also invest in other sides of the offer (price, service, lead times) as well as marketing methods (communication, information, organization). They actually develop or prototype their market in parallel by doing this.

- We make a distinction in this book between technological innovations and new products. New products are defined as products made to target customer expectations and needs. They're usually anticipated and welcomed by customers because they replace existing products that are deficient or inadequate. The innovation they bring is said to be "incremental" because it improves on existing products. On the other hand, technological innovations are developed at their suppliers' initiative, so their sudden appearance on the market has a tendency to take customers by surprise and disrupt their usual purchasing and work routines.

REFERENCES

Booz, Allen & Hamilton (1971). *Management of New Products*. New York: Booz, Allen & Hamilton Inc.

Bradley, F. (1991). *International Marketing Strategy*. London: Prentice Hall.

Callon, M. and Latour, B. (1985). Comment Suivre les Innovations? Clefs pour l'Analyse Socio-technique. *Prospective et Santé Publique*, 24 October.

Calori, R. (1991). *The Business of Europe Managing Change*. London: Sage Publications.

Chapelet, B. and Mangione, C. (1995). *Le lancement d'un produit nouveau*. Paris: Les Editions d'Organisation.

Choffray, J.-M. and Dorey, F. (1983). *Developpement et gestion de produits nouveaux*. Paris: McGraw-Hill.

Clugston, C.O. (1995). High-tech demands own new-product plan. *Electronic News*, 4 December.

Foster, R.N. (1986). *Innovation: the attacker's advantage*. London: Macmillan.

Grawitz, M. (1986). *Lexique des sciences sociales*, 3rd edition. Paris: Dalloz.

Latour, B. (1989). *La science en action*. Paris: Edition La Découverte.

Mansfield, E. and Wagner, S. (1975). Organizational and strategic factors associated with probabilities of success in industrial R&D. *Journal of Business*, No. 48, April.

Martinet, A.C. (1983). *Stratégie*. Paris: Vuibert.

Millier, P. (1987). Processus du déroulement du projet technologique. Research document IRE, January.

Millier, P. (1989). Le marketing de l'innovation technologique – eléments pour une approche non-diffusionniste. Research document IRE 9021, PHT.

Millier, P. (1993). *L'union chaotique du marketing et de la technologie dans les projets de recherche et développement*. Thèse de doctorat en sciences de gestion, Université Jean Moulin, Lyon III, February.

Rogers, E. (1976). New product adoption and diffusion. *Journal of Consumer Research*, **2**, March.

Silem, A. (ed.) (1991). *Encyclopédie de l'économie et de la gestion*. Paris: Hachette Éducation.

2
Major Marketing Problems in Technological Innovation

In Chapter 1 we tried to define the concept of technological innovation, to get a clear view of it and decide exactly which types of innovation project were addressed by this book. If you look at a large number of innovation projects over a long period of time you will note that they are often prone to the same pitfalls and mistaken reasoning. Although people in charge of projects are unaware of this, it's actually the errors made when thinking out projects that lead, slowly but surely, to their failure. But unfortunately it's often too late to make backtracks when you find out just how far you've gone wrong. In this chapter we deal with how to recognize the kind of pitfalls you can come across in innovation, and how to avoid them.

The first thing that comes to our notice is how an extensive range of project applications can make you so enthusiastic and so muddled that you end up:

- Developing devices instead of developing products
- Believing in the myth that a big market well and truly exists
- Blaming fate to explain your failure.

TOO MUCH POTENTIAL

There's one feature common to practically all the technological innovation projects I have been able to observe, and that is their initial potential. This potential concerns a wide range of applications and also seems to be a distinguishing factor between real technological innovation and mere product improvement.

You invariably come across the same phenomenon, whether you're dealing with the research centres of big industrial groups or with self-employed inventors. The people who carry these projects consider (often justifiably) that their product or technology has some universal relevance. And they base this claim on the apparent fact that − judging by the enthusiastic reactions of the customers they first approached with the idea − their product meets a great number of existing needs.

For example, someone who invents a product that eliminates bad smells can imagine a long list of possible applications. There are restaurant bin smells to get rid of, tobacco smells in cars or stale sock odours to deal with, smells from rubbish dumps or water treatment centres which need masking. You can easily find two hundred potential uses in one single brainstorming session, and your list will still be far from exhaustive.

Likewise, inventors of expert design systems know they can help customers design their products better, faster and more economically by memorizing specific customer knowledge. This system has endless potential because it applies to all areas where something is designed (aircraft, cars, air conditioning, machining, control systems, etc.).

There's one problem that often arises in this kind of situation. Inventors have one idea for an application, then another. That still isn't enough, so they organize think sessions and get a hundred more ideas. Then the clients' ideas are added on to this already long list of ways to go. But the longer the list is, the more complicated things get because the risk of being sidetracked increases. The fact is that you don't realize the risk involved because your list only lengthens a little every day or every month. You mark out your territory a bit further each time, unaware of the actual extent it now covers since all you have is a list of uses. And a list obviously can't give a meaningful picture of the market. All the problems on it are of equal importance and status and all of them are interchangeable. They have no particular links to connect them, no order of importance to differentiate them.

Take, for example, a project that we shall call "ultra-thin glass wool". This is a very fine, soft, silky type of glass wool which looks like cottonwool. The inventors jump to the conclusion that you can put their product wherever you put traditional glass wool or cottonwool. Their list gradually gets longer, with the following ideas:

- Cylindrical panels for aircraft insulation
- Glass wool blowing in roof spaces
- Artificial padding for anoraks
- Air filters for industrial fumes
- Blotters
- Cushions, pillows, quilts
- Carpeting
- Babies' nappies
- Cottonwool buds for ear cleaning
- Compresses
- Sanitary protection for the incontinent
- Pads for urine analysis samples
- Battery separators for cars or lorries
- Ear-plugs
- Soilless tomato-growing.

Not surprisingly, inventors tend to fluctuate between bouts of enthusiasm and confusion when faced with potentially endless lists like this.

TWO REACTIONS TO A PROJECT WITH STRONG POTENTIAL

Enthusiasm

Inventors may overenthuse when they see their product can be used anywhere. They certainly don't want to miss out on *the* market of the century, won't neglect any openings and think it's bound to become an all-purpose product for all applications, if improved on. Alas, the long, monotonous list is just a foil to real facts facing inventors. What they really need is an overall view to help classify the snags involved, and to show them that these problems need tackling in quite different ways.

What would they see if they had this overview? They would see their project sending off shoots, multiplying and mushrooming out. And they would observe the phenomenon shown in Figure 2.1.

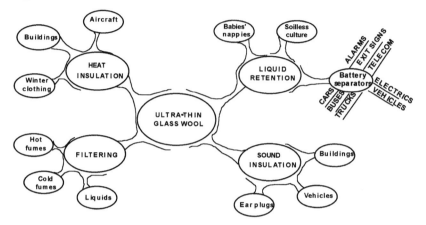

Figure 2. 1   *Example of project proliferation.*

Unlike the list that we started off with, Figure 2.1 actually groups and classifies possible uses according to their related problems. These groups represent the main fields potentially concerned (absorbent materials, heat insulation, sound insulation, filtration). A simple classification like this already shows that one initial project (ultra-thin glass wool) is going to branch out into four. It's obvious that problems connected with absorbency, heat insulation, sound insulation or filters are so different that they need individual research. But still further analysis would reveal that problems are not all of a kind even within one particular group. Take heat insulation, for instance. To insulate inaccessible roof space you need to blow fibre, which should float up, featherlike, then fall and settle evenly in mattress fashion. On the other hand, the fibre in anoraks should form a pad and hold together sufficiently for the wool to stay in place and give equal protection to the shoulders and lower back area.

The problem is different again with aircraft. Aeroplanes take off, fly at high altitudes, land. This means they go directly from temperatures of $+20°$ to $-50°C$. They also cross damp air layers which condense according to temperature variations. But glass wool soaks up this condensation and adds an extra load of

500 kilos on each trip because it has good water-retention properties (they're even thinking of making nappies with it). That increases aircraft weight and thus limits the payload. What's more, glass wool conducts heat when it's full of water, which is the opposite effect to the one desired. So research will have to be done to make the fibre water-repellent.

It becomes clear from these examples that the heat insulation project for ultra-thin glass wool will need to be subdivided again into three different development projects. And the more you look into it, the more diversified the problem seems to get. To give an example, the apparently unique battery-separator[1] application poses entirely different problems according to whether the batteries equip:

- Cars, which require a short power surge four times a day when starting up
- Fork-lifts on shopfloors, which empty their batteries during the day and recharge at night
- Emergency exit lighting, where the batteries are being charged continually with low-intensity current so they never run down
- Satellites, which need lightweight batteries with 100% reliability throughout satellite lifetime.

There are so many differences, implying so many specific constraints in battery insulation, that it would be necessary to develop one type of insulator per battery type. Only when you have this overall view do you realize that your one initial project would soon be subdividing into four, then 12, then 72 (or even more) small development projects if you wanted to follow up all these potential openings.

Overenthusiastic inventors or research workers who want to go everywhere run the risk of getting sidetracked and losing a fortune. What really costs a lot in Research and Development is person-hours. And the more the project diversifies, the more person-years that makes. But no companies have unlimited resources, so the only way you can do it all is to do just a little of everything, with the result that you eke out your money

---

[1] A battery separator retains the acid contained in the battery. It should let through the current but inhibit the movement of the acid.

between a host of small studies which never really get you anywhere and fail to deal with the real problem because you never reach its critical mass. There's a lot of beating about the bush. When you try to advance on all fronts, you don't make progress on any.

Confusion

Confusion is the other reaction I have seen to apparently boundless potential. Companies get buried under all the information they would need to collect, then deal with, then make decisions about and the longer their lists grow, the more they panic. Inventors or research workers are usually unfamiliar with marketing studies and don't know what approach to take. They don't know where or how to get information. No clear, quick, practical method exists for processing this kind of data, and there are no instruction sheets or criteria to help class and select what's most worth while for you.

The result is that you don't make any choices out of fear of making the wrong one. You let the project ramble on without any real strategy. Promising project seeks problem to solve! Decision maker seeks decision to make! (Cohen *et al.*, 1991).

You try out all directions and the project gets out of hand, with dwindling resources. Chance tends to lead the way. People on the project may get carried away unawares, though quite willingly, with the complicity of a customer who doesn't mind doing tests. But you don't know if there's a market to follow when you get carried away like this. You run the risk of heavy expenditure and have no guarantee of any investment returns. It can cost as much to do research for one customer as it does for a whole market.

The risk with this dangerous strategy is that you may end up sheltering behind technology, pretending to ignore applications. And what's likely to happen then? For instance, metallurgists who develop fibre to reinforce concrete will get to know everything about its metallurgy and characteristics. They will know all the alloys you can use to make it and their mechanical resistance, all the manufacturing parameters, the reactions of the metal when attacked by any acid or oxidizer, etc. In short, they'll have the best metal alloy on the market. But the day when a contractor asks them how much fibre you need to put in your concrete to reinforce it, they won't have the answer. Although they know the related technology they don't know how to apply it, which, you have to admit, is a real drawback to selling a product. From this kind of description you can sense what's coming: devices that are matchless in performance but completely unsalable.

THREE MAJOR MISTAKES IN REASONING

My observations have shown me that the enthusiastic or confused reactions described above lead to three major errors in thinking. All three are fatal because all are based in part on ideas that mean sure failure for the project. But these ideas are never actually questioned.

Devices

The enthusiasm that sets you looking for the all-purpose product for all applications or the confusion that drives you into hiding in technology can both result in what we shall call "devices" (Davidow, 1986). Devices of this kind are there because they represent the race for technical performance for performance's sake and because what can do the most can inevitably do the least as well. These devices carry the myth of Technology-that-sells. Above all, to use an old adage, they stand for "the best" which is "the enemy of the good".

To understand how you can fall into the device trap, let's see what happens when a project or an innovative idea first comes to light. To begin with, the company gives its project a certain "trajectory" which corresponds to the line of research in hand. Then, after a while, and several tens of thousands of pounds later, it starts wondering how to best make money with its technology. In other words, it tries to find applications. At this stage, everything's in the balance. If the company continues to develop its project according to purely scientific and technical logic as before, Figure 2.2 shows what may happen.

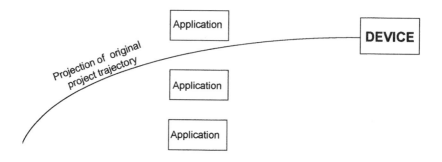

Figure 2.2   *Development process of a technical device*

The company runs the risk of bypassing applications entirely and developing a product that has no real applications and no potential buyers. This is the point where you can say that the company thinks it has developed a product, whereas in fact it has only developed a "technical device". Technical devices are the outcome of hard work by the company's technical departments (i.e. R&D, engineering office). They are designed and defined with scientific and technical rigour. But they don't account for customer requirements. A pressure gauge with precision of up to 10^{-9} bars would be a good example of such a device in the chemical industry, where the precision required is never more than 10^{-2} bars.

Technical devices are like products, but they're not products insofar as they fail to meet potential buyers' needs. You could complete this description by saying that technical devices are devices with unnecessarily high performance levels that you keep trying to sell to people who don't need them, either because they don't have any use for these performance levels or because they want them for something else. For example, customers in the chemical industry want their pressure gauge to resist high temperatures and corrosion, but they don't want 10^{-9} bar precision.

The difference between a technical device and a product is that a product stems from the joint efforts of a company's technicians and marketers. Strictly speaking, a product can be defined as the point where available techniques meet potential customer needs, either by chance or through concerted effort.

By comparison, the product process can be illustrated as follows in Figure 2.3. What this figure implies is that companies should start taking their end-users into consideration early on in the project. If you change course slightly while there's still time, you have at least some chance of succeeding because this is how you give the customers what they're looking for. The following example concerning electronic calculators is a good illustration of how a slight change of course can transform a device into a product.

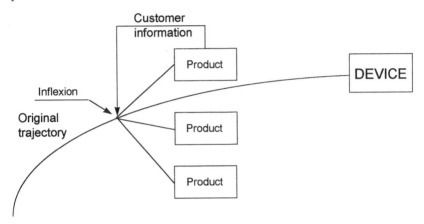

Figure 2.3   *Product development process*

The story took place in the 1970s. R. MacKenna (1985), an American consultant, was approached by calculator manufacturers who wanted to know how to make their product stand out from the rest. So he went to a store to see what customers based their choice on. He saw one customer who hesitated for a long time over two models that the salesman showed him, comparing them from all angles. One had Polish notation and the other hadn't, which didn't help the customer to make up his mind. The first one cost £425 and the second cost £475, so prices were comparable, and they both had hyperbolic cosines (which all of us need every day, of course, for personal or professional reasons...). But there was no decisive factor to guide his choice. So which one do you think he took? Believe it or not, he took the one that was heavier! What advice could the consultant give his client now? To make the calculator heavier, of course, by inserting lead batteries. This is a typical example of a marginal improvement that sells. It's marginal because it has no bearing on the basic principles that underlie the calculator. And it's just a detail. But a detail that pays off, since the customer felt that you got more for your money when you bought the heavier one. Now, in fact, nine times out of ten, research workers will find it much more exciting and rewarding to develop calculators with hyperbolic cosines incorporated than to put in lead batteries. But, unfortunately for them, customers never do use hyperbolic cosines.

Theoretically speaking, all this means that "devices" are probably responsible for four of the major causes of failure when launching technological innovations. First, companies think they have launched a product when in fact they have only developed a device. Second, by the time they realize this, it's too late to go back because that would cost them a hundred or a thousand times more. Third, some companies that have unwittingly developed devices persist in sinking money into their project in the hope that they will soon "hit the target". But if they reallocate the same budget without evaluating the situation better, they simply end up with a more clever second-generation device and then an even more clever third-generation one and so on (Figure 2.4). Fourth, if companies feel sure they have a leading-edge product and that technical performance sells, this will convince them they have access to a large, steady, safe, quantifiable market. And they will set out to conquer it under a complete delusion. We shall call this the myth of the big market.

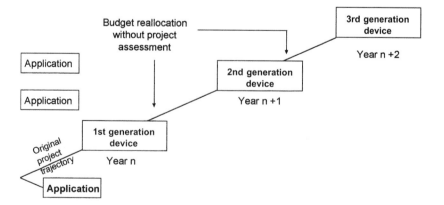

Figure 2.4 *Successive generations of technical devices*

The Myth of the Big Market

How does the myth of large, ready markets actually come into being, and how can you tell when you're falling into the trap? Let's go back to some previous examples and imagine what the inventors might be saying to themselves.

My pressure gauge has 10^{-9} bar precision, so it's the most high-precision gauge on the market and therefore the best one out. I'm going to be able to replace all existing gauges on the basis that what you can do the most with you can also do the least with. That way, I'll have the whole precision measurement market at my feet!

The metallurgist will argue that all you need to do to reinforce your concrete is to mix metal fibre with it. This avoids stocking and handling steel reinforcement rods which are heavy, dangerous and take a long time to put in place. In fact, the metallurgist thinks fibre is bound to replace steel rods because it makes concrete even stronger and decides that the whole reinforced concrete market is there for the taking. And the manufacturers of ultra-thin glass wool might just as hastily announce that the cottonwool market is their market too.

These three examples all have a point in common in their definition of the market. The innovators imagine the market is theirs and think of it in single, vague, all-embracing terms. But you may be sure you're on the brink of the large, ready market trap as soon as you hear yourself saying you "have the entire market" in, let's say:

- Tri-dimensional measurements
- Computer-aided whatever-it-may-be
- Global positioning systems
- Corrosion
- Sealing systems
- Absorbent materials
- Random signal generators
- Pressure gauges
- Reinforced concrete
- Cottonwool
- Thermoplastics
- Ceramics, etc.

It's obvious you have fallen prey to the big market myth as soon as you start singling out your market by referring to the chief function of your product (e.g. absorbency, positioning, measurements) or by naming the main product that's in competition with it (e.g. cottonwool, ceramics, thermoplastics).

The trouble is that you're looking at the market from a product perspective, not from a marketing perspective, when you define it uniquely in terms of your own field. From this angle it's easy to have the illusion that just because you have a unique, uniform product you also have a unique, uniform market. Similarly, if you define your market in terms of your competitor's market, then you are simply describing a market that grew up around a satisfactory offer (like cottonwool or ceramics). You can have the mistaken impression from this that their market, too, is as uniform, as straightforward and as unique as the product they sell. Unfortunately, this kind of reasoning isn't uncommon. You have only to look at the BCG or McKinsey-type strategic tools available to see that most of them put strong emphasis on competitor ranking, and thus encourage the tendency to compare.

But you're making a serious mistake here by focusing your observations on the offer and not on the demand. As Porter (1985) reminds us, it's dangerous to analyse markets from the competitor's standpoint because in fact, in their analysis, your competitors may well have forgotten or omitted to include the very elements that give your product its specificity. And since the characteristics of your product and theirs don't tally in all respects, this means that some segments of the market that are open to them will not be open to you. On the other hand, you might have access to markets that they don't have access to.

You can illustrate these relative positions as in Figure 2.5. In this figure you can clearly see a competitive zone between cottonwool and glass wool. But you will also see that cottonwool is going to maintain its own particular market. Likewise, there are markets where glass wool will have an unquestionable advantage over cottonwool. Saporta (1989) gives us an equally good illustration of this mistaken thinking when he tells how a large amount of marketing analysis is focused on offer rather than on demand out of sheer facility. Let's take the case of reinforcement fibre to show the sort of errors to which facility can lead.

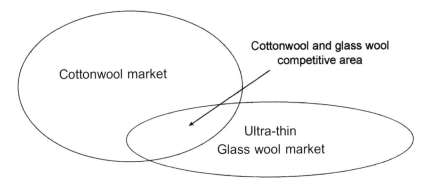

Figure 2.5 *Respective markets of cottonwool and glass wool*

One way to approach reinforcement fibre markets would just be to do a quick analysis and then say "I already know my market is the reinforced concrete market and that you need 3% of fibre mass in your concrete, and that concrete contains 30% of cement. So all I have to know now is how much cement is actually sold if I want to know how many tons of fibre I'm going to sell. In fact, I'll be selling a ton of fibre for every ten tons of cement sold. And because the amount of cement sold is equal to the amount of cement manufactured (since they never throw it out), I'll simply have to go and see the three or four big national cement producers and the customs authorities (to find out the import and export figures in cement) and I'll know my market after just a couple of telephone calls."

You could conceivably apply this analysis to reinforcement rods, too, if you decided to make them. You would go and join the continuous flow of products that guides suppliers towards new customers. But, alas, your product is not steel rods. The characteristics aren't the same, either in performance or in the way it's used. So its applications are not the same. As from there, you can no longer claim the reinforcement rod market is yours, too.

If you really want to target the specific market for your fibre the only way is to lead an enquiry directly with construction companies, public works contractors, builders. This is the opposite approach to soliciting cement manufacturers, and the focus here will be on market demand, not on market offer.

In fact, it's by analysing the largest possible number of

unsolved reinforcement problems that you're going to track down the weak points in steel rod market defences and detect chinks by which you could penetrate. Above all, you will discover the diversity of the market and be able to use it to your own profit. Cliffs, for example, are too dangerous and too costly to reinforce because non-professional climbers have to weave wire mesh over the sides before they can begin to project concrete. Another example is the renovation of main drainage systems. This is always a tricky problem because roads are up and traffic is affected for weeks on end. Contractors seek to overcome these difficulties by reinforcing the drain network from inside but space is very restricted and it's impossible to accede. The ideal, and unique, solution would be a gun to project concrete and ensure reinforcement at the same time. Next you realize what a boon it would be for airport constructors if they had heat-conducting runways to offset snow and ice in winter. Or you find people who just don't want their concrete to crack any more. There are even architects who would like to be able to make thin, very curved, very resistant walls for spherical houses.

If you hunted a little you would discover that reinforcement fibres solved many problems better than reinforcement rods do. But instead of telephoning three cement companies, you would have to visit 30, maybe 50 or 100 public works or building contractors, some drawing offices and architects to reach the result you're counting on. It's a long and costly approach, yet it's the price you must pay for finding out your market. And, whatever problems you may have with methods, it will make you aware of an even more important reality in industry. The fact that suppliers don't only have to interface with customers. They must analyse and cope with markets and whole sectors.

Why are Large, Ready Markets a Myth?

What allows you to think that large, uniform markets, which are there, which you can quantify, are a myth? They're myths in the sense that they are not necessarily of any interest to you on a long- or short-term basis, so in fact they are just expensive, elusive decoys. There have been many cases to prove that products which are "just a little better" than petrol or "just a little cheaper" than petrol usually have great difficulty securing any real share of the market in the short run.

To explain this, you need to go right back to the origins of the market. There has to be a demand before there's a market and this demand must be funded. But there's an essential phase before the actual demand. This phase can occur by chance or through concerted efforts, and market offer and market needs have to meet there. What does this really mean?

Let's go back about 15 years or so and try to imagine what users would have said if they had been questioned on their hi-fi requirements. They would probably have wished they had a better sound, discs that didn't wear out and an easier, quicker way to find the tracks they wanted. But not one of them would have asked for a laser CD player, because these didn't exist at the time. Laser CD players (originally invented for computer memories) coincided with user needs. But we must be careful here. It isn't because users were waiting for such a product that "Sony did it". In fact it's the other way round. The same reasoning could have been applied to microwave ovens or cellular telephones. Nobody asked for them twenty years ago because nobody offered them.

From what has just been said, we can schematize the phases of market construction as shown in Figure 2.6. According to this logic, what the offer does is to reveal the need by enabling customers to express a demand. Henceforth, marketing will consist of trying to make offer and need coincide so that customer reaction helps you to adapt your product. You can see here how far we are from the basic idea that marketing is restricted to revealing pre-existing markets. Seen this way, marketing actually leads to creating new markets.

When you look at Figure 2.6, though, you also realize that if a big market already exists there must also be some longstanding technology around to satisfy most customer needs. Otherwise the market would not have developed to that extent. The fact is that large markets have taken a considerable time to reach maturity in most cases. This implies that satisfactory technology is longstanding technology that plays an integral part within a highly organized technical system. For example, reinforcement rods for concrete have been here for a long time. Builders have learnt to work with them and are equipped to use them.

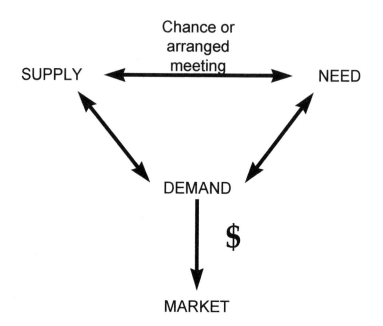

Figure 2.6   *Schematic arrangement of market-producing concepts*

So there has to be much more than just a little extra performance or a little less cost to dislodge existing technology, because customers know they risk losing a lot and don't know what they will really gain by switching technologies. There will have to be references and proof brought in to guarantee that the innovation will work from the word go and make money, too. Customers are already satisfied, unready to make concessions and unwilling to put up with even the slightest teething problems on a new technology. Experience proves that first attempts to apply innovations always raise a host of unsuspected problems. The fact is that big, ready markets are a deceptive lure for unwary innovators who don't tread the ground carefully beforehand to spy out possible openings. A better way to understand the risk entailed in this kind of situation would be to imagine the disaster that might have befallen concrete reinforcement fibre if the manufacturers hadn't taken the slightest precautions.

The adventure began in the laboratory, where it was tested and found easy to use. All you had to do to reinforce your concrete was to mix fibre with it. The resulting concrete was very strong and evenly reinforced. Once the manufacturers were convinced it would work they made a trial offer of their miracle product to a building firm. "You just need to mix it with the concrete, and that reinforces it!" What's more, there were none of the usual problems with steel (danger, difficulty, implementation time, etc.).

But it's a tradition with builders to mistrust new techniques because they have seen others. However, with a little luck and perseverance, the fibre makers eventually managed to root out a cooperative building firm which let them leave their bag of fibre and promised to try it later.

Left to their own devices, the builders didn't take any precautions, thrust their hands into the bag and promptly cut their fingers. From then on, they just loved it! Having donned gloves, they threw a few handfuls of fibre into the cement mixer. But the cement mixer wasn't adapted for fibre, so the handfuls stayed in lumps. They turned into hedgehogs which congregated around the blades of the cement mixer, and the blades got bent as they turned. The product had no shortcomings at all!

So now they had to scatter the fibres one by one in the cement mixer. This took ages, but the nightmare wasn't over yet. The fact is, they were using the same concrete as usual, with exactly the same composition as usual, but the fibre made it too dry. More water was necessary. Unfortunately, they added too much water in proportion to the cement so air bubbles and cracks formed in the concrete when it dried. This meant it was actually less well reinforced than it would have been without the fibre. The builders had had enough. But when they removed the shuttering and saw fibres sticking up in sharp spikes all over their new wall, it was the last straw. They just couldn't bear the sight of it, threw out the bag and cursed the day someone left it with them.

The innovators believed they had solved the steel problem but in fact they had unexpectedly raised a dozen others. And each of these problems was an additional and permanent deterrent for the builders. After all, they had never asked anybody for anything and were quite happy with the rods they'd been using for the last 30 years.

Don Quixote out to Conquer America

Although these examples are quite realistic, they do give the impression that you have to be very naive to believe in the myth of big, ready, uniform markets. Yet it's important to know that many industrialists have already experienced the computer science or telecommunications syndrome. What is this syndrome exactly? One of the stories began with an unknown hero called Steve Jobs, munching apples in his shed, and it ended with a worldwide computer market worth billions of dollars. Here is another. On one side of the picture there's Graham Bell trying to devise an apparatus to communicate with his deaf wife. On the other, there are vast telecommunications markets. The screenplay is always the same. Some obscure, hardworking inventor has an ingenious idea that opens up huge markets. You have the photo "before" the anti-dandruff lotion and the photo "after"; you have the market "before" and the market "after" the invention.

But these fantasies about inventors tend to blind us to the other 99% of reality. We don't see all the successive stages that come between inventors and large markets and this clouds our view of all the difficulties encountered, alliances formed, subsequent discoveries added to the initial product, discouragement, comings and goings needed to achieve this result. If you view situations retrospectively the perspective is flattened and those years of doubt and hardship when the product was striving to get a foothold are no longer visible. You forget each stroke of luck that helped your product come closer to a need you never imagined. That was how the diesel engine took over 40 years to become a current part of industry. As Latour (1992) put it: you only see the market when it's completed; you don't see it developing.

Yet we just have to look at Figure 2.7 to see that the telecommunications market wasn't built in a day. The fact is that the market is still under construction. It's gradually being set up through the efforts of industrialists, under pressure of their offer. But the Don Quixotes who go out in vain to conquer the big market haven't usually thought about this concept of setting up the market beforehand. As they see it, the market already exists. One good product will be enough to reveal it and a few good salespeople will raise the veil that's temporarily hiding it. The

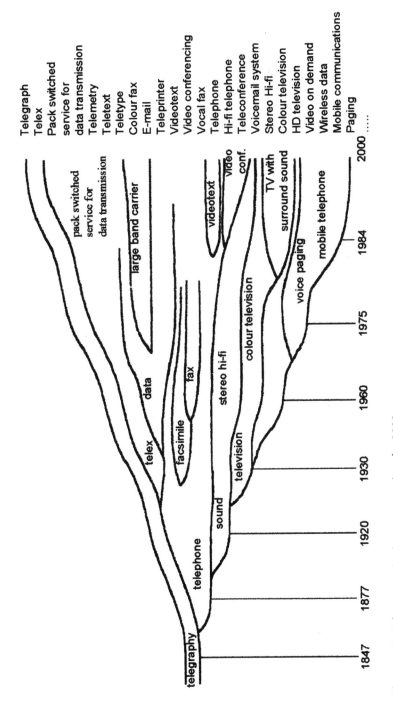

Figure 2.7 *Telecommunications: perspectives for 2000.*
Adapted from: Rapport sur l'état de la technique. Science et techniques, Special Issue, March 1985, p. 102

myth about conquering America is a very resistant one. Don Quixote set out to conquer the market in much the same way as Columbus went off to conquer America. But the difference between them is that America was there well before Columbus was. He didn't have to create it.

You could say that industrial innovators discovering their markets are a bit like builders, but builders without plans who only gradually get to know the shape of their houses, because the architects keep changing their minds as the houses go up.

As a last comment on the myth of big, ready markets, we can cite Paul Hawken (cited by Peters, 1988) when he warned the president of Exxon that people confused launching out into a business that would grow big with creating big business. It's a fact that the higher you go in big company hierarchies, the more yes/no decisions there are. Either the market exists and you invest, or it doesn't and you stop everything. There's no room allowed for midway situations where markets that don't exist could be created.

But we must never forget that the broadcasting market was not J.C. Maxwell's idea. He only invented the theory of electromagnetics. Markets can sometimes keep a surprise in store for their precursors, and markets will sometimes shape our futures more than we shape theirs. Generally speaking, though, ideas for products spread more readily than markets do.

Blaming Fate

The third risk you run with a technological innovation project is in fact the upshot of the first two. It consists of blaming your failure on fate. When they have developed their technical devices (as previously defined) and are beginning to realize that the big, uniform market just isn't there, innovators will start saying their failure was practically inevitable. But these are only alibis and false escape routes to avoid admitting they don't know why they failed.

What is fate? It's a mentality that grafts itself onto the minds of people who talk about it, blocks their powers of reasoning and paralyses their activity. "It's like that; that's just the way it is and nothing, no one will change the situation!" The danger with these ideas of fate is that they grow to be basic facts of life which no one ever questions, as "everybody's always said that and so it must be true". They are beliefs, unshakable inner convictions and accepted ideas because they "stand to reason".

Fate usually strikes as follows:

1 My product was ahead of its time on the market.
2 My product arrived too late on the market.
3 Some situations are just meant to succeed, but unfortunately that isn't our case. We don't have Sony's image and we don't have Thomson's resources. Our customers aren't any help and our suppliers keep letting us down at the last moment. The personnel lack motivation. What we need are some top innovators, but we haven't got any. Our industry is a disaster area. The customers have run out of money and you can't get any more subsidies from the government. There's Japanese competition everywhere.
4 Good products succeed and poor ones don't. There's a natural selection process and you can't do anything about it.
5 You have to wait for the market to open. Some markets are going to open and you just have to be there at the right moment.
6 Customers resist change. They aren't interested in innovation. Everybody knows farmers, builders and other blue-collar workers are against it.

But these ideas should be entirely rejected because they inhibit, block and ultimately kill innovative energy. As soon as you decide that nothing more is possible, you stop. Let's try putting forward some arguments to show these so-called fatalities are groundless and just make easy alibis when clichés take over from careful reasoning.

We can argue against them as follows, by claiming that:

• There isn't such a thing as a product that's ahead of time or behind time. A product is only ahead of time until the right set-up is there for it, technically speaking. A product is only behind time because it was developed in ignorance of existing competition. Take concrete reinforcement fibre. If added to traditional concrete, the fibre hardens this type of concrete too much for blending purposes in the cement mixer and the mixture is too thick to go through the pipes. The system won't work until you change the composition of the cement to make it more fluid, or reinstate an old technique using a dry process that consists of first blending the dry substances (i.e. cement, gravel, fibre), then sending them by air pressure to the nozzle region where water is incorporated. By doing this, you not only solve a technical problem, but you also make it possible to apply fibre. Technically speaking, you create the right set-up for the fibre. If you didn't, the reinforcement fibre would stay ahead of a market that might never open except perhaps at some competitor's initiative.

- No situations can give you prior guarantees of success or failure. You can be big, rich, do R&D, make a product that's not in line with what you usually do, be unfamiliar with the market, but not one of these is a characteristic either of success or failure. Every single case has to be described, analysed, understood, so you can then take steps to change and improve it until it succeeds. You can't expect to know the market for your technological innovation right from the start because it doesn't exist yet, but this doesn't mean failure. On the other hand, it's suicidal to launch a product without making any prior investigations. You're not in a hopeless situation when you don't know your markets, but you have to do something about it.
- No products can give you prior guarantees of being good or bad. As Callon and Latour (1985) say, no product is born good or bad. All products are equally bad at birth, but some of them become good because you fit them to customer needs. That's how the diesel engine, a poor product to begin with, achieved success after many person-years had been spent on its development and application.
- There isn't such a thing as a market that opens up on its own. It would be logical to claim that markets open according to how much vigour you put into opening them. The more you promote, the more you inform and the more your innovations will be requested. And the more successful experiences customers have, the better the grapevine will work and the more demand will grow. In other words, it's pointless to wait for markets to open. At the very worst, if you wait, they won't open. At best, your competitors will already have seen to opening them and they'll have outstripped you.

- There's no resistance to change. The fact is, there's no resistance to change that resists analysis. When customers resist change, it's because they have reasons.

You only need to see all the previously described disasters happen once to some builders (cut fingers, broken cement mixer, spike-covered wall) to understand why they have resistance to reinforcement fibre. But now we have found out the problems, we're in a position to seek ways of breaking down those barriers between builder and fibre, whereas just shrugging and saying "there's resistance to change" is tantamount to accepting that "things are like that and won't alter", which is simply an alibi to avoid admitting we don't know why the builders resist.

There's a way to save the situation once you have spotted your customers' motives for hanging on to old techniques or refusing new technology. But unless you find these underlying motives, it will be impossible to do anything about them except say "There's nothing I can do; the customer resists'.

Morin (1980) confirms this when he says that using a truism like "your daughter doesn't speak because she's dumb" to explain something only, in fact, expresses your ignorance of the problem in hand. You think you have explained the phenomenon merely by naming it.[2] He goes on to say that people are not systematically against change. No one would actually be loath to having a 5% pay rise. On the contrary, people willingly accept any changes they view favourably. They don't react irrationally from some basic anti-change, anti-innovation principle. When they're against change it's simply because they see the potential drawbacks of the innovation.

Morin groups these drawbacks, as customers see them, into three categories:

- Tiredness (duration, effort, monotony)
- Organizational constraints (procedures, time schedules, restricted independence)
- Constraints of rank (obeying, being judged, under orders or manipulated).

---

[2]   It's what is known as "substantive rationality".

He has likewise inventoried three categories of advantages which more or less compensate for the drawbacks:

- Salaries, perks (prestige, power)
- Good team spirit
- Interest in work.

Finally, he suggests that innovations won't succeed until we master the organizational constraints that represent 50% of the overall problem. Innovations can't succeed unless companies can learn to see things the way individuals do.

It should be realized that giving up ideas of fate or fatality amounts to giving up the easy ways out and the passive attitudes they encourage us to have. Once you have rid yourself of this onus, your mind will be a lot freer to try to understand how the market actually works and which strings to pull. Understanding the market means you can control its opening and you can control product diffusion.

It isn't a question of simply going along with the market as it is. Quite the opposite, it's a question of provoking market reaction. In this way, you reverse cause and effect: instead of adapting to market evolution you induce it in order to benefit from the resulting impetus. The idea is not to find and follow a flourishing market but to make one. And appropriate steps need to be taken to open it up. In short, it's not the market that is going to shape you. You are going to shape the market. After all, flourishing markets wouldn't be there without us. Marketing doesn't consist of raising veils on existing realities (i.e. markets), but of actually helping to build them.

Checklist

- What most technological innovation projects have in common is promising potential. They give the impression there are countless applications. Projects mushroom out as they develop, sending out ever-branching clusters in different directions. The first step you should take here is to fully describe, and thus circumscribe, your field of applications.

- Project managers tend to be either enthusiastic or confused when they're faced with this proliferation of ideas. Over-ambitious companies get sidetracked, driven on by enthusiasm at the prospect of so many potential project applications. They try to develop the perfect all-purpose product that will satisfy everyone and end up with an all-in-one product, the sort of device that doesn't satisfy anybody. In contrast, other companies with muddled methods and no helpful criteria will choose their application quite arbitrarily. Not only do they risk coming to a dead end, but they may miss more worthwhile openings in doing so. One especially pernicious type of "opportunity" consists of letting yourself be inveigled by a particular customer into developing the product that customer needs. It's sad to say, but that customer may be the sole person who needs it, and additional demand non-existent. You risk spending as much on one customer as you would on a whole market.
- There are three seeds that sow destruction for 95% of all technological innovations:
  - Developing technical devices instead of products. Technical devices are research items with outstandingly high performance levels that companies keep trying to sell to customers that don't want them. Outstanding performance is more of a handicap than an advantage and again brings home the fact that technology isn't enough to sell a product.
  - Believing a big, safe, uniform market, one that can be calculated in figures, exists out there for your very clever device – and going to look for it. The big, safe, uniform, ready market everyone looks for can justifiably be called a myth until you actually test your product on it. In fact, whenever you think you're solving problems you are usually just raising a dozen other unexpected ones that undermine your chances of launching the product directly. It's much more reasonable and realistic to consider that technological innovation markets are composed, initially at least, of many non-related segments.
  - Blaming fate to explain failure. This stems from a rather fatalistic attitude that it's pointless to discuss, but which

impedes action. The seeds of destruction sown by fate differ from ordinary failure factors because they induce the reasoning which leads to failure without anyone realizing they do. Misled thinking like this consists, first, of believing that markets already exist and that innovations bring them to light and, second, that technological innovation and performance are bound to sell.

REFERENCES

Callon, M. and Latour, B. (1985). Comment suivre les innovations? Clefs pour l'analyse socio-technique. *Prospective et Santé Publique*, 24 October.

Cohen, M., March, J. and Olsen, J. (1991). The Garbage-can Model in Organized Anarchies. In March, J. (ed.), *Decisions and Organizations* (French edition: *Décisions et organisations*. Paris: Les Editions d'Organisation).

Latour, B. (1992). *Aramis ou l'amour des techniques*. Paris: La Découverte.

MacKenna, R. (1985). *The Regis Touch: New Marketing for Uncertain Times*, Reading, MA: Addison-Wesley.

Morin, P. (1980). Réponse au refus du produit nouveau. *Revue Française de Gestion*, January–February.

Peters, T. (1988). *Thriving on Chaos: Handbook for a management revolution*. London: Macmillan.

Porter, M. (1985). *Competitive Advantage: Creating and sustaining superior performance*. New York: Free Press.

Saporta, B. (1989). *Le Marketing Industriel*. Paris: Eyrolles.

3
Basic Rules of Marketing to Answer Specific Problems

The previous chapter gave us some idea of how to recognize and avoid the main pitfalls for innovation. Avoiding snares is a must. However, skirting all dangers is a strategy without being one, hollow strategy based on what you mustn't do, not what you must.

Now is the time to bring in some basic marketing rules as guidelines. They will answer the problems raised previously and show us how to ford the turbulent transitory phase prior to launching. This implies getting to know all the marketing tactics you need to implement before the product goes into its commercial life-cycle.

Prior to this, you should let your project proliferate and express its potential. This will give you a wider range of possible targets before you finally decide on what to focus your energy.

A TWO-PHASE ANSWER: PROLIFERATION AND FOCUS

What these basic rules can give your innovation strategy is something more than just a static view of the project and its applications. For instance, it was a static image of ultra-thin glass wool that we gave in the previous chapter (Figure 2.1). Although the static view does have to be built up, it is still not sufficient to manage a project. It has to be taken further. What we need is a dynamic picture of the project, one that moves. This is where our marketing rules could be summed up in two words: proliferation and focus. To begin with, that implies letting the project proliferate, drift, widen its perspectives. Then, during a second phase, it means making a choice and keeping to it, to avoid dispersion.

You could compare proliferation with breathing in and focusing with breathing out. First we breathe in or inhale, then we exhale. But the essential point to retain from this comparison is the continuity of the process. The cycle never stops. You don't take one deep breath at birth and then let the air out gradually for the rest of your life. On the contrary, right through life we are going to have a regular breathing rhythm. This could be an image of our continuous efforts to widen the scope of our innovation project, so that at any given time we have a larger range from which to choose our application.

The technological innovation management process is rather like a film where you alternately zoom out and zoom in. Zooming out helps you to visualize the general picture so that you can spot interesting details to zoom in on. When you widen your field of observation on a regular basis, it's easier to decide what you want to see in close-up.

Proliferation and focus follow on from each other and together form the transitory state between research and launching that we spoke about in Chapter 1. We can now give an initial picture of their positioning with Figure 3.1. Let's use an example to help us interpret this figure correctly.

Imagine you are developing a non-destructive ultrasonic laser control system. This technology is in its infancy and no salable products have been designed with it yet. All you have is some vague research prototype. It's an assembly of lasers, optical components and reflectometers which are adjusted down to the micrometer, and it lies on a marble surface, safe from any temperature variations, vibrations or dust. You are in phase one. At present you're trying to demonstrate that the system can generate ultrasonic waves in a part by means of a laser.

Then you test the product on the market (i.e. marketing becomes involved in the project process). At least 50 potential applications come to light, including:

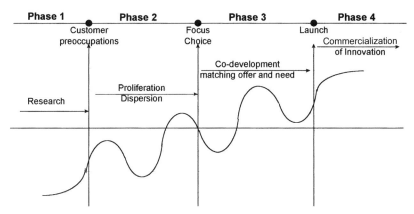

Figure 3.1 *Transitory state*

- Controlling rails on railtracks
- Controlling high-pressure pipelines
- Controlling blanks from the roller-mill
- Laboratory control of composite materials
- Controlling large parts for the boiler-making industry, etc.

Starting from here, the project is liable to grow and branch off in all directions. You are in phase two. All this potential has to be explored to some extent before you analyse the comparative risks (see Chapter 4) and choose the most accessible short-term application: laboratory control of composite materials. Then you confine your efforts to developing it for several months. This is phase three. At the end of this phase the initial product is ready to be brought out. It's still a sophisticated product, hard to get the right settings with, costly, geared for research personnel, but it's the only one that can identify flaws in composites to such a high degree of precision. So you launch your product on the industrial research laboratory composite control market (e.g. aeronautics, cars, sports equipment) and you go into phase four.

So far, you have pursued a proliferation-focus process which has culminated in the launching of a given product on a given market. Now, if you want to launch another non-destructive ultrasonic laser control system on another market, you will have to repeat a similar process. And start off all over again with a long list of potential applications, taking care to add on recent finds as you go along.

When you pick the best short-term application you must bear in mind what the odds are from a sales perspective and what you've learnt from composites. Then focus on it until you're ready again to launch another product on another market, and so on.

PROLIFERATION

Chaotic Proliferation

The proliferation phase is the time when projects are put to the test on the market and undergo changes, with customers adding on elements that research never had in mind. It's also a creative phase when you start to find product applications. So much the better, too, if unexpected applications do turn up. The project will be all the more enriched. Jacques (1990) reminds us that a vast number of great inventions, including things like the telephone, aspartam, and nitrocellulose, were actually brought to light through applications they weren't planned for at all.

During the proliferation phase, projects tend to go off in all directions and generate new market constraints that can be a hindrance to proceedings for some time. One way to express this would be to say that projects enter a chaotic phase. They send out different offshoots, as we saw with ultra-thin glass wool, and these offshoots branch out again in their turn. Projects bifurcate or mushroom out (Figure 3.2).

Van de Ven and co-authors (1989) note that: "When the innovation begins to play an important role in the company, the new idea enters the proliferation phase and diverges in lots of directions. This divergence can be seen from all the non-related products around that are based on the initial concept. Products which needed quite a few more ideas and improvements to become what they are."

The chaotic phase begins with marketing. Projects enter an exploratory phase, then proliferate because they are stimulated by the discovery of whatever is vaguely or supposedly

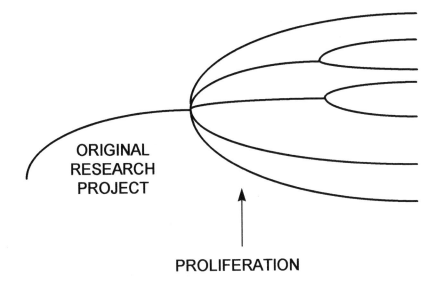

ORIGINAL
RESEARCH
PROJECT

PROLIFERATION

Figure 3.2   *Proliferation*

applicable. You don't finalize anything during this phase, nor do you look for any solutions. But you explore. You widen your field as far as possible in order to have the biggest choice of applications you can. There might always be a sure route to success but if you try only one path your chances of finding it are sorely limited. This phase is essentially a creative phase in the cycle but you have to go further to get any benefit from it.

Let's not be mistaken about the meaning of "proliferation" here. You might well be afraid of going completely off track. But this isn't the case. Proliferation doesn't consist of developing your product for each potential outlet. It just helps to open doors so that you can see if there's anything interesting behind them. In practical terms, proliferation can begin by a wave of creativity then continue with a small exploratory market survey to test whether such and such an idea for an application is of potential interest to customers. For instance, you will investigate to see what unsolved problems they have with their particular non-destructive control system.

Once you have made quite a systematic survey, you will have a single, structured picture to help you classify and rank your potential markets. This original way of visualizing markets is achieved by using what we call segmentation (for more details on segmentation techniques for non-existent markets see Millier, 1995, and Chapter 4).

There are all sorts of chaos in the proliferation phase. Chaos can come from inside or outside companies. It can be due to the project or independent of it. It can be destructive or constructive. About 30 projects were followed over a period of several years to bring this diversity to light. Preliminary marketing studies had been carried out on all of them. These projects give us some good illustrations of what chaos can be.

Examples of Chaos outside Companies

- There's a sudden call for tender on a European project, and the company is obliged to restructure, get organized, set its objectives, fix lead times and make commitments. The call for tender will be quite a constructive factor and give the ultrasonic laser control project its initial impetus.
- Socio-economic changes, changes in industry, politics or the environment, changes in standards, regulations or taxes can suddenly force new choices on you. Projects may have to be reorientated up surprise channels. For example, the battery-separator project came to a halt in 1988 because of a price war in the United States. But the American battery-separator firm then responded to the onslaught of its new US competitor by finding a partner in Europe who could cut transport costs. The new partner was already well implanted on the market, so this enabled the American company to get a good foothold. External chaos was constructive here. In the tubular membrane filtration project, the chief potential partner was a subsidiary. But its head company was disinterested in it, viewed it as a misfit. Paradoxically, another group spotted some strategic value in the project and bought out the subsidiary. At long last this group had found a way to get into high-range food product filtration via the subsidiary. So the project took off. Constructive chaos again.
- Opportunities arise or doors close when competitors appear or disappear. Take CVD machines, for instance. Chemical vapour deposition is the process used to make electronic substrate. When Japanese competition turned up, the supplier managed to obtain government subsidies for customers who bought the

domestic product. External chaos paid off in the end. As for the heat-transfer fluid project, this was launched after the main domestic competitor withdrew from the market. Outside chaos was constructive once more. On the other hand, the belated discovery of a paralysing patent can stall your research and stop you developing your innovation. This is obviously a destructive factor if you don't try again some other way.

Examples of Project-induced Chaos

Project-induced chaos can take the following forms:

- After initial tests on a special measuring computer, first sales, press reports and advertisements, customers took the company by storm with requests for servicing or information and brought the organization to a complete standstill. The company obviously had to react quickly and reorganize itself to meet this situation.
- Disastrous results like breakdowns or accidents are extremely negative factors when you're initially customer testing your product or have just made your first sales.
- One day, out of the blue, a customer buys a large number of products for testing purposes. It's an unpredictable order. Nobody knows if it will be renewed or what the customer is going to do with it.
- A company creates demand by the information it diffuses and the contacts it makes. But it can't satisfy this demand – at least, not on a regular basis – because of limited means of production. This creates a sawtooth pattern of production–storage–consumption variations (Figure 3.3). In this case, chaos is engendered by the company's incapacity to regulate demand.
- A customer who regularly makes the same purchases suddenly stops ordering, without giving you any warning or reasons.
- A major partner turns up for your product. An example of this is the filtration membrane project, where customers suddenly saw strategic value in participating in the project's development.

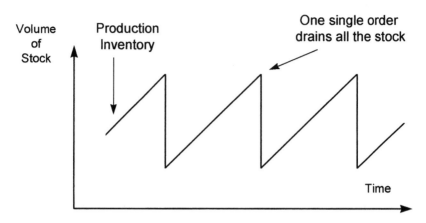

Figure 3.3   *Sawtooth diagram of production–storage–consumption cycle*

Some Examples of Internal Chaos

When things are shifting outside a company, chaos can also appear inside it. The two phenomena are not necessarily related, but most of the time internal chaos has repercussions on external chaos, and vice versa. In other words, the project influences its environment and the environment influences the project.

For instance, internal chaos occurs when projects disperse in a lot of directions at the same time. Overactivity is a form of internal chaos. Then again, upheaval can stem from marketing surveys with disastrous results that imply on-the-spot decisions to stop projects or to radically reorientate them. But it's also frequent for projects to cause dysfunction, internal blockages that are visible from disputes, basic disagreements, people snubbing each other, creating slippery situations for each other, or standing by principles that always seem to end up in arbitrary decisions.

The following are some practical examples of what internal chaos can be like:

- The research team on a special optical-fibre project was heading for some interesting results in performance levels (in attenuation at very long wavelengths), when it was disbanded and another team formed. But the new group never managed to get more than half the performance level of the first team.
- During a project on research equipment, a violent confrontation broke out between the project leader and research

workers concerning objectives. Only when the project manager resigned did the conflict come to an end.

- The partners in the measurement computer project had a misunderstanding over initial choices. Finally, the head research centre had to intervene but the choice they enforced was quasi-irrelevant.
- The sales partner in an electronic circuit project had obtained exclusive rights to product diffusion. But the product was then deliberately stifled because it outshone the sales partner's own products.
- A new director made a lightning decision to stop a "smart building" project because he "didn't believe in it".

But fortunately internal chaos doesn't always end in disaster. Marketing often brings very constructive chaos as soon as it becomes involved in the process, either through market studies or when innovations first brave the market. In fact, market studies often coincide with radical changes in company attitudes towards projects. People start making major decisions about changes in project management methods.

- Here is one example. The research leader in the reinforcement fibre project gradually switched to project marketing, took on outside promotion of the product and handed its development over to technicians. He travelled the building sites to keep a close eye on fibre implementation and devoted most of his time to marketing.
- Here is another example. Once they had completed the market survey for their composite material project, the innovators could focus on three segments. The research project then turned into a development project, led with the help of operational units from the company group.

Company management can sometimes start supporting a project that only a few research people believed in until then.

- The tubular membrane filtration project got company backing in the end when the firm realized just how interested one of their very big industrial partners was. ("If X is interested in it, it must be worth something.")
- The battery-separator project aroused management interest as soon as a partner was found to help penetrate the car market.

Finally, the following are some examples when organizational changes in project management can induce chaos:

- When you're setting up subsidiaries
- When you're setting up sales subsidiaries
- When you're working with experts who trade their customer files
- When you're collaborating with operational personnel from the group.

Basically you can say that chaos is constructive when it helps things to fall into place, and destructive when projects never recover from it. But although these observations are interesting and useful they leave one big problem unanswered. The present state of our knowledge is such that we just can't predict whether chaos is going to be constructive or destructive.

Effects of Chaos

From the research-related projects given, we can infer that chaos usually means projects are going to change or that project management methods are going to change. Companies are obliged to make other choices if they want to keep their projects under control. So when projects switch from research stage to development stage this causes discontinuity in the project management process (e.g. team changes, changes in management rules, changes of status).

Chaos sometimes implies high levels of project instability. Projects are fragile in themselves. They can be torn one way then the other by decisions. Decisions that may have nothing to do with the projects, but still influence them. (For instance, the company goes into debt to finance its external growth, and reduces its research budget by 20%!)

The examples we looked at previously were good illustrations of projects in tug-of-war-type situations.

- The "smart building" project was indeed stopped by a new director who didn't believe in it.
- Many conflicting decisions were made about the special measuring computer, with each partner tugging in a different

direction. Specialists were brought in from the research centre to solve the deadlock between the two company members. Their databased decision was final. But it wasn't unanimously accepted and the project was divided up again. In the end the software suppliers walked out on the project.

- The research equipment project bounced backwards and forwards like a ping-pong ball between the orders of an authoritarian manager and the research team, who wanted to make a product in line with customer requirements.

But instability phenomena occur in successful projects, too.

- For example, they stopped the battery-separator project because costs were too high and demand was too low. Then it came back to life after a market survey revealed that competitors had withdrawn from certain markets.
- About two years after it first came out, the reinforcement fibre project took off again on an entirely new basis, technically speaking.
- The ultrasonic laser project was radically reorientated towards spectro-photo-thermo-acoustics not long after a market study had been done on it. But the main thing was its contribution to a call for bids by a government ministry. For political reasons, this call was withdrawn at one point. But later, after government re-election, the call for bids was reissued and the budget renewed.

You can also see how unstable projects are by the extent to which they depend on initial situations. The effects can be immediate, either positive or negative.

- The reinforcement fibre project was "launched" thanks to its initial application to the drainage system in a main provincial city. The innovators managed to instill confidence in the project with the first full-scale test, and it took off.
- The battery-separator project recovered after being brought to a standstill. Why? Because there was a price onslaught by US competitors against the very people who were to become the project's partners in the automotive industry.
- The project on tubular membrane filtration started looking up as soon as an industrial partner came along.

On the other hand:

- Although the composite material project got off to a good start, it suddenly ran aground when a customer had a major implementation problem.
- The measuring computer project collapsed when PCs came onto the market.
- The special optical-fibre project came to an end when there were changes made in the team. The new team just couldn't match their predecessors' performance.

Whether its positive or negative, the fact is that chaos has an immediate effect (i.e. success, failure or reorientation) on the future of projects. Projects may outlive chaos or they may not but they never come out of it without changing, one way or the other.

The Necessity for Chaos

Chaos means disorder to a lot of us and we have the impression that disorder is rather harmful. It calls up hostile environments we should try to avoid or keep well clear of if we do have to face them. Curiously though, innovation projects seem to need this chaotic phase. Out of 30 projects studied, all the successful ones went through a period of chaos. In contrast, projects that went smoothly right from the start all foundered.

It seems clear that chaos during the proliferation phase is a must for product success. But it's only one of the requisites, because there were also failures with some projects that did experience chaos. In fact, chaos was so devastating in those particular cases that it killed the projects outright.

If you push the analysis a little further, you see that chaos has to be both internal and external for the project to succeed. It all happens as if internal chaos was the response (or echo) to external chaos. When things start to move outside, then things have to start moving inside. Project and environment carry out a sort of mutual adjustment through this echo effect.

If you continue thinking along these lines, you will note the failure of all projects with an isolated development: that is, those that had no outside impact. This seems to imply that chaos is not the sole condition for success. What you can infer, though, is that the environment must react to the disruptive effect of innovation if the project is to succeed. Theoretically, from these observations, chaos alone is not enough for success, but absence of chaos is enough for failure. To sum up:

- Absence of chaos is enough for failure
- Destructive chaos is enough for failure
- Constructive chaos is necessary, but not enough, for success.

The following are two metaphors that help to illustrate how and in what way innovation actually benefits from chaos and makes use of it. The first is a game of Lego. You already have two houses in Lego (i.e. environment and innovation) and you want to make a castle with them. But you can't just pile them one on top of the other. The only way to manage is to break them up (partly at least) and put them together again in a new order. An innovation can't evolve well in an environment that already has its own particular structure, unless innovation and environment undergo some kind of prior change.

The second metaphor concerns the mixture of two solids. The way to make a particular alloy from two solid substances (A and B) is by melting them, mixing them and solidifying them together. You start off with a certain order (i.e. two blocks of a different substance), you create disorder (or chaos) by melting them, then you achieve a new order which is different from the first (i.e. the alloy). The new substance has properties that are not the same as A's or B's and the resulting product can be said to transcend A and B (Figure 3.4).

If you look at it from this angle, putting a technological innovation on a market where nobody's waiting for it is tantamount to creating havoc. The upheaval disrupts the existing

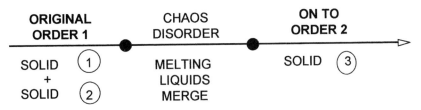

Figure 3.4 *Essential role of chaos in creating new order*

order of things, to which the innovation doesn't belong, then sets up a new order that includes the innovation.

You cannot overemphasize the importance of chaos during this phase if you want your project to succeed. Latour (1992) wrote about this in *Aramis ou l'amour des Techniques* where he tried to understand the failure of a domestic project on a cellular public transport called Aramis. This was his conclusion: "[The project] Aramis has been the same for the last seventeen years. Nothing has changed. There haven't been any sceptics or any hitches. When it dies, it will be as complete and as fresh as when it was born. . . . But, and here is the snag . . . Nobody talks about it. Everybody is buzzing away inside the Aramis mobile but outside they're like stone statues." In other words, the Aramis Project didn't create any external chaos, which is one of the reasons why it failed.

During project evolution, random technical concepts start springing up "by chance" in large numbers, almost as if it were a natural process. And the more diversity there is, the more chances there are of finding true applications. The most important point to notice, though, is that project management methods change during this chaotic proliferation phase. Projects are thrown in a whirl when people start discovering potential fields of application. Until then, research had just been trying to get to know the technology. Now it's possible to imagine applying this technology, finding answers to something with it.

The basic conclusion you can draw from this analysis is that chaos is essential to a project's future, and if it doesn't turn up on its own then you have to make it turn up. As we have already seen, market surveys usually have sufficient impact on projects to improve their chances of succeeding. Perhaps smooth running is more pleasant, but it always leads to failure. A time comes when you must stop cringing in front of negative customer impact. You have to face it, even if you get a good hiding.

Ed McCracken (in Prokesch, 1993) underlines the need to induce chaos. His company's philosophy, he said, was that there was no competitive advantage from reacting to chaos, only from provoking it. And he specified that the key to making chaos was to be an innovation leader. You only have to reverse the order of Ed McCracken's comment to say that the key to being an innovation leader is to provoke chaos. In all the successful cases studied, chaos always enabled innovators to force the lock that held up project development, whether they knew what was obstructing it or whether they didn't.

FOCUS

Concentrating Your Energies

When you talk about "focus" in innovation projects, you are referring to something very specific. Focus here means selecting a few applications or market segments (between one and three, according to your finances), then devoting your entire energies to solving technical problems, one by one, as they come along, until they have all been solved and the product is ready for launching.

Focusing on one segment has basically the same effect as focusing with car headlamps. All you need is a modest 50 watts to see very well at night a hundred metres ahead in the light beam. Nothing on either side though. You have to spotlight the important area. Forget about the rest.

Hence focusing implies concentrating all your energies on a choice in which you have complete confidence. Then it implies persevering with that until you succeed, going at something unswervingly until you have reached your goal. It's also true that when money is limited, concentrating it on selected segments means you increase its usefulness. So focusing is also a way to avoid dispersing your resources and eking them out unproductively to fund a lot of different project ventures. Basically, it means setting your mind on one particular thing and sticking to it.

The need for perseverance just cannot be stressed too much because focusing on a project can sometimes be enough to discourage even the most stubborn of us. Everything is fine as long as you stay in the research laboratory. The project goes ahead at an encouraging pace. But later on, with increasing customer application to real-life situations, there are more and more snags. And it takes time to sort out these minor problems, so that hoped-for horizons seem to recede as you advance.

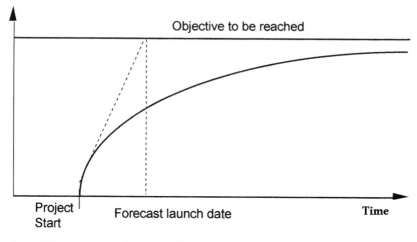

Figure 3.5   *Increasing divergence from goal trajectory*

This paradox, said to be Zeno of Elea's, can be illustrated in Figure 3.5. When horizons grow further and further out of reach like this, it is loosely translated in companies as the π(Pi) factor, meaning that innovation projects always last three times as long and cost three times as much as planned. Diesel learnt Zeno of Elea's paradox at his own expense about a century ago. He wrote something like this to his wife on 3 October 1894:

> At the beginning of the year I got nearer to my goal than I thought I would. Unfortunately I then took another direction in the hope of improving results. So now I must get back to my February figures, and complete them (from Thomas, 1996).

Once he had solved the main theoretical problems, Diesel really believed he had hit the bull's eye with the first prototype, available in August 1893. In fact, the engine was very underpowered and had to be rebuilt. In the end, he needed more than four years to make it work just about adequately. Four years of unrelenting effort.

> Diesel hoped the development process would be quick because he had decided that he shouldn't resort to any fundamentally new techniques (Thomas, 1996).

He had no inkling of how many difficulties he would have to overcome.

> High-pressure rates and high temperatures generated by the engine caused valve leaks, leaks at joints and in the cylinders, as well as rapid parts wear.

Diesel and Augsburg both had access to the traditional know-how of the machine industry, and could apply to it for help. On the other hand, the second series was entirely new, in spite of what Diesel said. What size should the combustion chamber be? What was the ideal fuel? How did you inject it? What was the right air–fuel ratio for the mixture? Diesel and Augsburg were working in the dark here. The only way to find answers was by meticulous experimentation. Diesel wasted time up blind alleys. He tried several different carburettors and fuels. He even went so far as to try different ignition systems. It's obvious he was ready to do anything, even to give up the idea of the compression-ignition engine At the beginning of 1896 the engine worked but there were still some major technical problems. The air-compressor caused several unexpected and highly dangerous explosions and the spray nozzle was constantly getting clogged up with residue. It took some years to remedy these two defects (Thomas, 1996).

Going from Research to Development

It doesn't seem much when put in these terms but, in fact, choosing one (or several) segments to focus on is one of the most important decisions in the entire process. This is the decision that propels the project into its development phase and shifts it to a new system of management once again. It has to be carefully planned because you need to be prepared for this new type of management and the changes in the project this will bring. You are leaving an exploratory research phase now, to enter a finalised phase of development. The changeover can be illustrated in Figure 3.6.

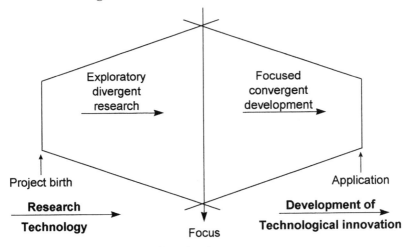

Figure 3.6   *Going from research to development*

These remarks about the difference between Research and Development are not just of theoretical interest. They should help us to realize that once you focus on one particular segment your project becomes another kind of project and so it needs another kind of management. It's not only the project that changes. The team should change officially too, at a functional level if not at an organizational level. From now on, development teams must interface with customer problems and explicitly incorporate them into the development.

You may remember that the reinforcement fibre project was named after the product's constituent right through the research stage. Then, when the project entered its development phase and the focus was on concrete reinforcement, the name became "fibre concrete". The team changed in this particular case, and a reinforced concrete specialist (an industrial client) joined it. This is a perfect illustration of the way a changeover like this in management methods can be made official; could even form a sort of ritual, which is what happens with product launching.

The expression "Research and Development" no longer makes sense from what we have just said. Because you don't do R&D any more. You either do research or development, but not both at the same time on the same item.

As we said earlier, focusing means going right to the end (i.e. to launching) unswervingly, without giving up at the first difficulty and transferring to another segment on the excuse that farther fields are really greener. The fact is, your efforts on the first segment may well be completely wasted if you then opt for another segment, because the problems there won't be the same. Everything has to be started from scratch all over again. You also risk meeting even tougher problems then you did on the initial segment, which means you will probably be trying a dozen openings at this rate and not getting anywhere on any. It's what you call jumping from the frying-pan into the fire. Drucker (1985) conveys the need to be almost stubbornly persevering in a good article called "The discipline of innovation". This article explains how efficient innovations begin quietly. They aren't grandiose. They try to fulfil very specific tasks. But, of course, no one can say whether innovations are going to transform into big business or just live on as modest accomplishments. Above all, innovating demands hard work, concentration and accuracy. All your talent, ingeniousness and know-how will be to no avail if you fall short of the mark in speed, tenacity and commitment. Drucker is obviously encouraging modesty rather than too much ego.

We have already mentioned one excellent example of obstinacy; the innovator in the concrete reinforcement fibre case, who had to:

- Find a way to stop the fibre cutting people's fingers
- Find a way to spread the fibre evenly without it going into spiky lumps
- Reintroduce an old technique for piping concrete in its dry form, to avoid piping the abnormally thick concrete, fibre and water mixture
- Find a way to prevent the fibre from sticking up when the shuttering was removed.

This case is clearly a good example of closer links developing between key elements in a project. In fact, the above-mentioned problems were all solved by adapting either the equipment or the concrete, but not the fibre. It was the fibre manufacturer who put the pressure on and contributed to developments in concrete and equipment so that the fibre could find a place in the public works and building industries. Not the other way round.

Focusing may seem the natural thing to do when you look at these examples. Yet it isn't a very natural step for project leaders. Focusing is equivalent to narrowing down your choice to a few specific segments and failing to explore others which might just have led you to the market of the century. This is why it's so frustrating for decision makers to choose segments to focus on. And why it's essential to have rigorous methods in marketing analysis (see Chapter 4), ones you have full confidence in, to brace you for these choices.

Let's look back at results from the 30 innovation projects. Some statistics from this detailed long-term analysis confirm the absolute need for focus if projects are to succeed:

- Four successful projects were focused on one market segment
- Seven successful projects were focused on two market segments
- Four successful projects were focused on three market segments
- Three projects failed although they were focused: two for technical reasons, one through failure of the sales partner.

In contrast, the other projects that dabbled with a large number of different objectives in parallel all failed without exception.

Focus through Co-development

Focus is associated with a joint development phase in the same way that proliferation is associated with a chaotic phase. In all the cases studied, each company focused on a segment in collaboration with customers who had some particular interest in joining the project. Ed McCracken calls his customers "scouts" and specifies that scouts are people who take two hours telling you what they would do with your product if it could calculate ten times faster, and how they would do it. People who just want a cheaper product, he tells us, aren't scouts, and he goes on to say that when you work with scouts you should learn what they are trying to do with your machines or what they want to do with them, and you should try to put this potential in an easy-to-use form in your new generation product. Von Hippel (1986, 1988a) calls his customers lead-users, and defines them as customers whose current needs will be generalized to the rest of the market in a few months or a few years. They're the clients who reap the most benefit from adopting leading-edge trends to meet their requirements.

You could also call them pioneer customers because both they and their suppliers are daring enough to accept the odds on innovations that are still very uncertain, whether they're promising or not. It must be realized that when customers actually commit themselves, they have little or no idea what the future holds in store. Their needs are seldom well defined and they don't know what impact the new products will have on their work, or how to evaluate them. Nor do they know where to get helpful information to judge them by, nor whether the products will still be around in a year's time. From their point of view, innovations can certainly be called a gamble.

A relationship is established between customers and innovators. Customers provide opportunities for full-scale product application and suppliers are able to take stock of all the running problems as they come along. It was at the very first building site where they used it that they noticed the reinforcement fibre cut people's fingers and broke their cement mixers.

But customers play a bigger role than this. The truth is that they end up with the best possible solutions for their problems by helping innovators to finish product development. Developing products in common like this can be called co-development. There are many big advantages for innovators in this system. Basically, the joint effort means they can share the brunt of development costs since customers are investing both time and money. But it also means that innovations progress in a far surer way because customers give the innovators guidelines by specifying their own particular needs. It's no longer a question of guessing what clients want. In other words, innovators don't take the leap on their own. They have their customers and partners alongside to help them.

The leader on the CVD machine project confided:

> You can never develop without a lead-user, and this is all the more true when the market doesn't exist. What we did was to pick a lead-user, a silicon-wafer manufacturing company, then co-develop the machine with it. These people bring in expertise, ideas and experience. [*Note*: The lead-user selected was a small, domestic wafer-manufacturing company which always actively sought to have cutting-edge technology.] We chose these people because:
>
> - They have some experts
> - Their customers see them as experts
> - They are geographically close, which makes communication and feedback easier
> - They are regular customers
> - They are very cooperative and full of ideas.

But co-development's real value lies in the mutual changes in customer/supplier attitudes. Clients gradually start to feel it's their own project as work progresses alongside the inventors. They project their problems onto it and contribute their knowledge. The development carries their hopes of an answer to a problem they can't solve. It means they invest even more and are less likely to give up on the way. And all this encourages the innovators to adapt their product to customer needs. Meanwhile the customers realize how they should gear their requirements to the innovation they are gradually coming to know, and exploit it to the best advantage.

This implies that suppliers make some sort of concession towards customers during co-development by adapting to them. That's one of the basic rules of marketing. But in the present case the customer also makes a concession to the supplier. The upshot of this is what you might call dialectical progression, a logical step-by-step process whereby each party concedes in turn by modifying its initial standpoint. This is how the customers' requirements evolve once they have grasped the full potential of the innovation, and this is why the product bought is not the same as the one the suppliers originally think they will be offering. Suppliers and customers can now be said to interact.

We can depict this gradual convergence of offer and need as in Figure 3.7. The figure shows how offer tends towards customer requirements. At the same time, these requirements evolve because customers realize there are better ways to take advantage of the offer. Offer and need are reiterated, and thus gradually converge until they meet.

Dialectic (according to *l'Encyclopédie Universalis*) is always linked to an idea of progression, of going from one term, or state, to another. No dialectic is stationary. Dialectic also has to do with a notion of reciprocity between the states it links together. It shows up reversals of situation and incompatibilities. It proceeds by means of objections, contradictions, questions and answers. And dialectic unfailingly ends in a compromise.

The following example is a good illustration of dialectical

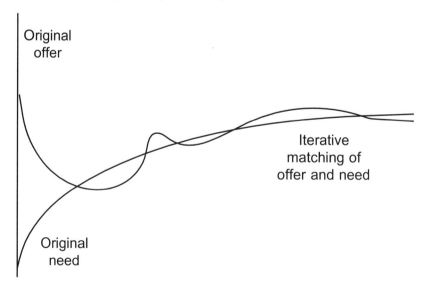

Figure 3.7   *Offer/need convergence process*

progression. In this particular case, composite materials are being introduced into helicopter rotors (i.e. hubs which support and orientate the helicopter blades).

To begin with, rotors were built from a large number of bearings, springs and forged machined parts which were either interdependent or jointed. The whole set-up was so complex and delicate that an hour of maintenance was required for each hour of flying time. As people are always seeking ways to lighten aircraft, a manufacturer offered to replace the metal parts by lighter parts in composite materials. Then the rotor manufacturers realized that these materials could be tougher than steel in one direction and more flexible than steel in another, so they completely changed the concept of their rotors. By rethinking the design with composite materials, they managed to reduce the 370 parts for the Alouette rotor (1955) to 202 for the Gazelle rotor (1970), then down to 70 for the Ecureuil in 1980. The outstanding Starflex rotor, with its supple, flexible, elastic head in a fibre-glass and resin composite, got rid of the high vibration levels on the mechanical parts. The advantages were: less weight, easy manufacturing, shorter production time, fewer parts to control, less wear, fewer breakdowns and easy maintenance.

When the rotor manufacturers agreed to modify rotor design, they benefited far more from the changeover to composites than if they had stood their ground. And this remark is equally relevant for some suppliers who flirt with failure by refusing to budge an inch from their initial positions, whatever it costs them.

Another advantage in co-developing a product is that customers sometimes think up new ideas for using it. In fact these new ideas are often much better than the initial ones because they come straight from the customer. They represent a wealth of new, self-determining markets that can save you many hours of prior assessment.

In addition, co-development puts project developers in touch with customer technicians. This direct relationship is a good way for researchers to actually hear customers contradict them and to admit they're right, since the problems crop up before their own eyes. They always find some sort of rejoinder, whereas in other circumstances they would tend to deny the problem if one of the company's sales department reported it to them (the general belief being that salespeople, by definition, know nothing about techniques).

This instantaneous repartee stops clients making a fixation on the problem and pulling down the product and the company in general. Nothing is worse than customers who try to get by on their own with a product which doesn't work well or that they aren't using properly. If you aren't around with your expertise and your motivation when the hitch occurs, then the problem will be your fault or your product's fault but never your clients'. Progressive troubleshooting will enable you to deliver a product that works and can at least reach the performance levels you said it would. And you will avoid giving your customers expectations you can't live up to. It's a fact that the farther you climb, the farther you will fall. And not only will the customers fail to forgive you; they will also give you a bad name.

Finally, co-development lures customers into an adventure that isn't too costly in the early stages. And according to the so-called commitment theory (Joule and Beauvois, 1987), people are even more committed by their acts than by their convictions. This tends to lead them on through thick and thin because of an initial choice.

In theory, though there's no clear explanation for this, people who have committed themselves a little are even prepared to make bigger commitments on the same score – as if to bear out their initial choice and legitimize it by proving they were right to themselves and to others. This would signify in the present context that clients who agreed to co-develop will be much more inclined than others to adopt the innovation and purchase the product later on.

So if you convince customers to commit themselves to co-development, you increase your chances of keeping them. That is, once customers have joined your project, they will feel it's their own in some way, and will try to defend it and to make it succeed at all cost.

A Good Example of Co-development

Brown (1991) brought us a particularly successful case of co-development when he recounted how Xerox developed a product for the pharmaceutical industry by collaborating work between their PARC (Palo Alto Research Centre) researchers and some of their customers' personnel. He said that the essential research partner with Xerox was the customer, that this was not to be confused with traditional marketing, where you assumed that the product already existed or that customers knew what they wanted in advance. On the other hand, from a PARC viewpoint, he said, you had to deal with systems that didn't exist yet and needs that still weren't clearly defined. Their objective was to help customers express their latent needs and then build systems that were perfectly adapted to these needs. This was why, before they designed a computer system prototype, they looked for a prototype of the actual needs or uses. He said they had already taken a step in that direction when they joined the "Express" operation, the research group launched with Xerox. This experiment aimed to speed up the marketing of technologies that came out of their laboratories by directly involving the customers in the innovation process. The operation, he continued, was carried out by a team of researchers, engineers and salespeople, together with some personnel from a customer called Syntex, a pharmaceutical laboratory.

Brown went on to describe how there were a thousand research workers optimizing new medications at Syntex. The Express team was studying ways to apply a technique developed at PARC to help the laboratory control some 300 000 "forms" a year that retraced the results of new experimental products on humans. The Syntex personnel did a course at PARC to learn the new technologies which had been developed there and the Xerox personnel led an in-depth study on work processes at Syntex.

Brown described how they defined the main needs of the pharmaceutical product manufacturer and the most appropriate PARC technologies for these needs, then came up with some prototypes. The team created a new system called the "Form receptionist", which read, sorted, filed the Syntex forms and used different techniques to distribute them, like scanning, document recognition, translation. He comments that the cooperation was doubly effective because Syntex solved an important management problem and Xerox perfected a prototype product they could sell to the pharmaceutical industry later on.

Aside from this experiment, the author said that the Express project was under study itself as a prototype of "coproduction" with customers. All discussions between members of the two companies were videotaped and processed to make a visual database, and he added that a second research team was busy thinking over the entire collaboration process and the lessons to learn from it.

The experiment, he said, made them realize how difficult it was to communicate and how long it took to have the team share a common language and common intentions. They therefore thought it was fundamental to find how computer science could speed up the mutual understanding process within a workgroup.

He said, in so many words, that the ultimate accomplishment of cooperation between customers and manufacturers could be a sort of prospective laboratory where Xerox clients would have access to advanced programming tools that would make it possible to model the consequences of the new systems they were planning to buy, and project these consequences into the future. This way, customers in contact with Xerox marketing and development departments could try out new configurations of the computer systems, assess their usefulness, streamline them and gradually fit them to their real needs. Then, the author declared, you would have a system producing new product simulations before the products were even created.

Some Real Examples of Collaboration

The following are some examples of the dialectical process taken from the 30 projects under study:

- Innovators and customers work together on a joint definition of the product.
- Suppliers and customers reciprocate by taking turns to adapt the innovation to technical needs, using a series of interactive tests which go back and forth between problems and possible solutions.

Suppliers and customers fix common objectives which take shape as new product potential is brought to light. This is the way new applications come into being, when customers look at the innovation and recognize specific potential.

Bearing this in mind, can we say, for example, that finite element analysis (i.e. a computer science method to calculate a structure by its mesh) existed before computer science? Or is it computer science, insofar as it's a calculation tool, that's behind the conception of FEA? Which came first, the hen or the egg?

Once objectives are fixed in common, suppliers and customers gradually optimize the innovation/technical need relationship until both parties are satisfied by the result. But there are often quite a few tussles before a compromise is reached, as witnessed by the following examples:

- Having to find a compromise between price and performance, a compromise between performance goals and old existing production tools, or between several conflicting technologies.
- Having to reorientate the project owing to a partner's demands or constraints. For example, this may lead to giving up performance research or characteristics research on the equipment, and dealing with machining or surface-related problems instead.
- Having to reorientate the project when the innovation first links up to a partner's technology.
- Having to get several different parties to collaborate in the development of a new thermodynamic loop system to carry a new heat-transfer fluid or to develop a new treatment system for fluids.

The Partners in Co-development

Who are the Partners in Co-development?

We have emphasized the customers' role in co-development. But we have to bear in mind that there are many people actively concerned by the introduction of the innovation, so co-development can happen on several levels. There are two large categories of collaboration:

- Upstream
- Downstream

Upstream collaboration is generally established with research laboratories. The objective here is to develop broader, more in-depth knowledge about your own technology. For example, you will have a whole series of measurements taken to trace the hysteresis curves on a metal substance to be used for magnetic applications. Or you'll have a series of measurements taken by a heat science laboratory to establish the heat capacity/temperature diagram for your heat-transfer fluid. This type of collaboration can take the form of a contract or gentlemen's agreement that satisfies all parties concerned. Companies develop their technology while laboratories develop their knowledge and publish fresh findings from the new experiments.

In contrast, downstream collaboration is established with different parties from industry with a view to improving the implementation of a particular technology or its transfer to customer industry. This type of collaboration can intensify to the point of becoming a real partnership where all parties are equally active. As a general rule, the partners come from customer industry and offer some complement to the innovation. Very often these partners want the innovation implanted in their industry for strategic reasons, or they can be partners you need as stepping-stones to the market. For instance, if you want to make glass wool battery-separators, then you will first have to work with the paper manufacturer who initially transforms the glass wool.

Partners' decisions can be motivated by strategic interest:

- The innovation gives them access to new markets
- The innovation is a way to improve their competitiveness
- The innovation is a way to overcome technical and economical restraints.

Partners can be clients who use their research and development laboratory as an intermediary. They can also be capital equipment manufacturers, who want to develop a special filtration unit with tubular membranes, for example. You also find industrial research laboratories like steel industry research institutes, for instance, which do the job of company R&D laboratories when these don't have the time, proficiency or interest to co-develop the product. They can work on the customers' behalf. You also get cases where "independent experts" work under contract on project developments.

Finally, there are inside partners. They can come from a company you have downstream. For example, it might be a public works contractor who could test your new concrete reinforcement fibre. Inside partners will always be preferable when you want your work to remain confidential as long as possible or when in-house use of your product is an outside reference because of the confidence you have openly expressed in it.

How Do You Spot Potential Co-development Partners?

Accurate and very detailed analysis of your sector will help you select the most suitable partners. You will generally look for partners in the areas where your techniques are most deficient. For instance, in the fibre reinforcement project, the initial developer was a steel company that chose to associate with a firm in building and public works. You can choose partners for their image, their references, the weight they carry in customer industry. For example, the non-destructive ultrasonic laser project was developed for composite material control through collaboration with Dassault, or Aérospatiale.

Sometimes you can't strictly speak about choosing your partners:

- For example, in France, there's only one possible partner for the non-destructive ultrasonic laser project in the steel industry: IRSID (the French steel industry research institute).
- Partners are self-determining (i.e. they come of their own accord and so they choose themselves).

More often than not, though, it isn't as easy as that to identify pioneer clients. Von Hippel says you can spot them among the precursors. Those who are on the cutting edge of technology as far as needs, new products and new processes go. He claims that lead-users are active innovators and that you can pick them out easily because most people in industry know who's doing research on a given problem. They can be persistently difficult to identify in spite of this because they are not core customers of the industrialist who's doing the market study. They can be competitors' clients or hail from a completely different industry to the one to which the innovation is geared. What's more, lead-users may just be interested in one aspect of the innovation and not the whole thing.

Another system for tracking down partners is to go through organized networks. If you want a confidential way to find a commercial, financial, industrial or technological partner, you can address the Business Cooperation Network (BCN). This is a network of some 600 business consultants who work in the public sectors within the European Community and in a number of developing countries. People wishing to offer or request cooperation can get in touch confidentially over the Net (Nehme, 1992).

What are Pioneer Customers' Motives?

Another clue to finding pioneer clients is to go back to customer motivation (people who adopt an innovation always have a motive), and lead on from there. Of course, this motivation still has to outweigh their interpretation of the risk involved. Fortunately, customers may have countless different motives. But you can find practically all of them in a list of nine, which was drawn up very empirically from a hundred or so market surveys. These nine types of motivation are the following:

- Production-related or technical motivation
- Sales motivation
- Competitiveness
- Financial motivation
- Social motivation
- Regulation-related motives
- Environmental motivation
- Strategic motivation
- Fashion.

Production-related or Technical Motivation

Research, that is, research on unique solutions for longstanding, severe or recurrent technical problems comes first on the list of technical motives. By production-related motives, we mean any motivation to manufacture better quality products, to instal a quality policy, to improve productivity, to maximize specific tool use, and to find other outlets for products made with that particular tool. You will find these motives among the company's technical staff in functions such as:

- Technical management
- Production management
- Methods
- The engineering office
- Quality control management.

They are the ones to target in your initial penetration strategy, by making it clear how the innovation can help each of them to do their jobs better.

Imagine, for instance, that you're trying to sell a noise analyser for rotating shafts to a quality control manager. Of course, it will help the customer company to improve the quality of their gearboxes. But this is only a meagre advantage as the quality manager sees it. For the quality manager, what counts is the tangible demonstration to everyone, superior management in particular, that the right person is on the job. We could also talk about those noisy green machines with scooter engines that go along domestic city pavements picking up dog excrement. Their primary objective certainly isn't hygiene, because they raise the price of the goods in question to £45 a kilo, which is round about what *foie gras* costs. So it's the mayor you need to convince here, not the people in charge of the streets. It will be a good publicity stunt at election time when all the work that's done to keep the town clean is being so brightly and noisily advertised. Find out who benefits from the crime. That's the way to discover motives.

Sales Motivation

For example, customers who are sales motivated will try to:

- Give better service to their own customers
- Make products their customers vainly keep asking for
- Reach new markets or new clients
- Change their image
- Increase their turnover.

Generally, a customer company's salespeople will have this kind of motivation. So you need to go and see your customers' sales or marketing manager, or the product manager, with arguments fitted to their motives.

Competitiveness

It's out and out warfare when customers are in a critical competitive situation. They will expect you to give them a competitive advantage or to offset their competitor's lead if the competitor is ahead. Usually the best way to open these customers' doors is to address their sales or marketing function. But first you must take care to find out what their warring is all about.

Financial Motivation

You could say that all customers have financial motives. This is true, of course, but in this particular case they have to be motives that incite the customers to take an interest in your product. Financial motives include:

- Reducing investments (i.e. producing as much with three machines as with two)
- Avoiding investment
- Reducing fixed assets
- Producing at less cost
- Increasing profitability
- Obtaining subsidies. (This is the case with research laboratories that have to officialize their collaboration with industry before they can get subsidies from supervisory organizations)
- Obtaining reduced insurance premiums.

This type of motivation is prevalent in various different functions. You find it in general management or production management. It all depends who has the job of cutting expenditure or making money.

Social Motivation

This mainly reflects the preoccupations of the personnel:

- Redundancies

- Employment protection
- Response to employees' demands
- Improved work conditions
- Prolonged company involvement following retirements and layoffs.

Human resource management is likely to be sensitive to this motivation, but so are hygiene committees and safety committees. Trade unions, too, can be negotiating partners. For example, this is the case in Italy whenever firms buy machines that could jeopardize employment or modify the type of work involved.

Regulation-related Motives

State enforcement is often a sufficient motive to channel company interest towards given products. This is a motive to look for increasingly if you're selling a product that can reduce (or eliminate) pollution, smell, noise, or environmental nuisance. You will meet the whole array of statutory obligations in standards, laws, decrees and restrictive circulars. But the hand that wields the stick can also give carrots in the form of tax incentives (like tax aids or subsidies).

Regulation-related motives can sometimes really shackle companies that have just been threatened with drastically worded texts like "If you don't stop polluting before the end of the year, you will have to close down!"

Environmental Motivation

This is what you call the "green spirit". You recognize this type of motivation when you spot services called Mr Pollution, Mr Waste recycling, Mr Environment, Mr... Quite apart from any ecological considerations they may have, some companies are limited by climatic conditions like rain or drought. For example, three years of drought can force a big power utility to instal a waste water recirculation system because there isn't enough water in the river. But whenever there's flooding it has to stock its waste water until the flood levels subside.

Strategic Motivation

These motives are linked to company strategy and generally concern company management of the branch or unit in question. You can consider they're implicit whenever managers:

- Fight shy of control by monopolies
- Specify supplier nationality
- Make efforts to diversify
- Seek to relocate.

Fashion

Fashion has surprising sway even in industry. If so-and-so is already equipped, then you can't afford to waste time. Any company departments may be implicated here. It depends what exactly the new fashion is about. For instance, computer-processing management will succumb to LANs (local area networks), marketing management will succumb to industrial design, and the engineering office will succumb to the trend for 32-bit microprocessors. . .

These are all reasons for doing things (and sometimes reasons for not doing things), and you hardly ever meet customers who are motivated by just one factor. And all these motives go together to form customer behaviour.

The Disadvantages of Co-development

Every medal has two sides and co-development sometimes poses a few problems. These include information leaks and ownership problems concerning the techniques that are developed.

Of course, you can insert a confidentiality clause in your collaboration agreement to avoid information leaks. That doesn't guarantee absolute protection but it limits the risk. On the other hand, Von Hippel (1988b) says it's usually better to talk than to shut yourself off. According to him, you save so much time gaining from other people's experience that you easily make up for any leaks in your own trade secrets.

As far as ownership of knowhow is concerned, it's not uncommon for partners to insist on sharing, or having exclusive rights. You can try to get round this problem in two ways, although you don't always have the chance to. One strategy is to refuse, arguing that there's another partner in the offing. This is a defendable position, because when people ask you for exclusive rights it means they are already afraid of someone else going off with them. You can also try to limit the extent of the restriction by granting exclusive rights only for a fixed period or within a limited geographical zone. All points have to be negotiated, one by one.

Three Basic Rules to Take You through Focus

As we have seen, you can use the chaotic phase to your advantage by opening doors and encouraging chaos to come in. Likewise, there are some rules for getting through the second transitory state phase. These are basic rules of management that specifically address focus in co-development. Three of these basic rules were identified thanks to our 30 sample projects:

1 Have an overview of your market
2 Act quickly
3 Take on weight.

First Rule: Have an Overview of the Market

You can't drive a car at night without headlamps and, in much the same way, it's impossible to lead your project to success if you can't see where you're going. This is why you need an overview of the market before you launch your offensive. It must be an original overview, in the sense that this is the first time the market has been viewed this way, and it should be all the more original because the product is innovative. But your overview will not be predictive. It's just a guide to help you stalk a moving target. Visualizing the market is a way of making it more intelligible to people navigating in the dark. Of course, this rule doesn't specifically apply to technological innovation in industry because it's also the starting point, explicit or otherwise, of any form of strategy. However, it's all the more critical with technological innovation to get a first coherent vision of your future activity.

This view can be acquired from market segmentation (see

Millier, 1995) further to a market study. The segmentation method helps you to determine the shape of your potential market, to divide it into uniform segments according to technical and behavioural descriptors (or explicative criteria) and to describe the segments you thus obtain. In a way, segmentation invents the marketplace then gives us a picture of it. This picture is a map that helps us locate ourselves on the battleground and launch our offensive at chosen targets. It's the basic document you need for decision making and acts as a navigational aid.

But segmentation isn't enough to give you a complete picture of the market. To complete the picture, you need an analysis of the sector to find out at which level to enter. Are you going to make steel slabs, forged parts, or machined parts ready for assembly? Then a diagnosis has to be made to help you eliminate inaccessible segments and concentrate on less risky ones. Diagnosis acts rather like a wide-angle lens, magnifying things in the foreground while those in the background recede.

Since this overview is supposed to indicate the repercussions of your choices, it should also incorporate any induced phenomena, any closed-loop phenomena. There are many closed-loop phenomena in emergent markets. For instance, it's impossible to estimate market size and dynamics without taking your own impact into account. Likewise, shrouded competition can come to light as soon as your technological innovation goes onto the market. The competitors are ready, but have no desire to disclose their intentions as long as nothing forces them to do so. So innovation is the agent that unveils competition.

You must also include the possibility of a closed-loop phenomenon when you assess price. Price is an integral part of the price–demand–volume loop, which can be illustrated as in Figure 3.8.

Technological innovation marketing is essentially based on the principle that new products have high technical differentiation potential. But it's also obvious, on some markets at least, that price exerts an influence on demand. However, demand influences price in its turn so you have another closed-loop phenomenon. You can't have an elementary, linear approach.

Whenever there's some degree of price elasticity, it's a fact that price brackets will condition critical demand level. If the supply markets can keep up (which remains to be seen case by

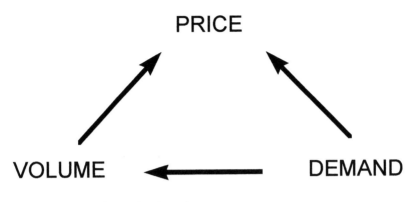

Figure 3.8 *Price–demand–volume loop*

case), then higher demand leads to an increase in quantities manufactured. But this increase in quantities manufactured can lead in turn to lower prices, and influence demand once again. This depends on the volume effect and learning curve (unless they don't apply to your technology under normal conditions of production). And so we loop the loop once more. You can sum this up as follows:

- Low sales price → high demand → large quantities manufactured → low cost price → low sales price...

If you change the premises, the reverse is also true:

- High sales price → low demand → small quantities manufactured → high cost price → high sales price...

Note: These ideas in no way aspire to being norms or an application of neoclassical economics. They are just meant to illustrate what a closed-loop reasoning process can be. And to show how choosing one particular item like price can influence several levels of a system that's made up of interdependent elements.

Project leaders testify personally to the importance of having an overview of the market. One day the sales manager on an optical fibre local network project told us: "The marketing study enlightened us. We saw what action to take and what choices to make. Before that, the technicians were left to their own devices. It was pot luck which customers they went to see. This study has helped us to focus our energies on real targets." The battery-separator project inspired a similar comment: "We got a good enough picture from segmentation and analysis of the sector to pick our future launch partner. Sector analysis is a reflex with us now." Or again, from the non-destructive ultrasonic laser project: "To begin with, we only saw the technological showroom side to it; we didn't have a clue about markets ... The marketing study was a revelation. As it happens, we concentrated on the two segments that were diagnosed to be the least risky."

Second Basic Rule: Act Quickly

It's imperative to act quickly as soon as you have a picture of the market. Marketing studies only give temporary overviews that are relevant when the studies finish but can evolve rapidly. If markets are in the process of adapting to an innovation that's still evolving they will undergo noticeable changes in the course of time. Customers no longer react the same way. Their needs change through exposure to innovations, and pressure from competition modifies the general outlook.

If you apply your 1999 view to the situation in 2001, it will be right out of line with the realities of the moment. And if you base your 2001 decisions on the view you had in 1999, any moves you make will be irrelevant, and so they will be the wrong ones.

This is what happened with the project on heat-transfer fluid. The biggest domestic competitor withdrew from the market. That radically changed the company's position. The firm went from great precariousness during the market study to a very favourable situation in the market, and product launching became feasible.

The tubular membrane filtration project could not get into the food industry market because the only conceivable partner would not collaborate. A little later this potential, but unavailable, partner changed hands and was taken over by a company in the food industry. The new head company radically changed the firm's attitude because they saw the project as an opportunity to get their grip on the elusive high-range food market.

A firm carried out a market survey for two years in a row on the use of chemical neutralizers in waste water treatment. But one segment of the market disappeared in the second year because waste disposal legislation had changed in the interim and customers had been obliged to become equipped with waste disposal units. There were no more potential clients for the neutralizers.

Third Basic Rule: Taking on Weight

If you want to ford the transitory state in optimal conditions you need to develop the structure of your activity so it gains in influence and importance. The bigger and more structured your activity is, the better it will resist internal chaos. The more people there are in your activity, the better it will weigh against complex company structure. The greater your commitments are, the more irrevocable your decisions will be. The higher your total net income is, the more credible your activity. The stronger your construction is, the better it will weather the storm.

But you can also get weight by taking on people from outside the company, by creating networks. Close links in networks like this help to consolidate a project's hold by encouraging its "external growth". Projects use this mesh of technical and economic links to find outside support and footing. It arms them better against chaos.

The Necessity of Focus

You can only really talk about crossing the transitory state when you are in the focusing phase. It's the core area of product development, because it's the phase where device and need begin to converge. It's also during this phase, under customer influence, that companies choose quite unforeseen channels and learn to bow to the constraints of their environment. This is the phase, too, where firms exploit their creativity. It's the dialectical fit-and-focus phase during which you concretize the project by fitting it progressively to its environment, and vice versa. Mangematin (1993) emphasizes the fact that you should view (and manage) this period as if it were a development phase. He writes:

> It's truer to say the first users are chosen by the suppliers than to say they actually choose the technology themselves. This choice is related to

supplier strategy. But the first users also play an active role because they actively participate in the conception of the technology and hold a position midway between the end-user and the developer. It's obvious the suppliers' choice of first users is an integral part of the development process for the technology. A choice which goes on evolving right up to product diffusion.

This gradual convergence phase is absolutely essential to project success. Latour (1992) testifies to this with some insistence: "The cellular transport system hadn't adapted to any environmental changes. It was a pure device, and a device which was pure. Miles away from people. Miles away from history. Completely isolated." Did they ensure the project could absorb the 600 four-seater cars necessary for an urban transport system? No. Did they take the project to another site? (It would have been more favourably implanted in a city without an underground railway system and big bus services). No. Did they increase headroom for standing passengers at rush hour? No. In other words, the project didn't fit the environment and the environment didn't fit the project. There was no dialectical process to make the "pure device" converge with the "public transport product" the customers wanted. Latour put it this way: "There was no feedback available on different locations or running systems to redefine the mobile."

MANAGING THE TRANSITORY STATE

Keeping Proliferation and Focus Together

Proliferation and focus are two complementary and indissociable stages. They are the ingredients of the transitory phase. And it's also true to say that successful technological innovation marketing means fording this transitory phase in optimal conditions.

We may be repeating ourselves here, but it's important to remember that proliferation and focus phases only run consecutively when you plan to launch a specific product on a specific market. However, if your project life-cycle jumps from one product to another, your proliferation and focus phases will run parallel with each other right to the end of project development.

Proliferation and focus are complementary, like breathing in and breathing out. Proliferation brings creativity, a large choice potential and outside enlightenment. Focus helps you to exploit creativity, to make something concrete out of it, to fit the project to its environment and the environment to the project. It makes them inseparable.

Both approaches are complementary. Try to go everywhere proliferation takes you and you won't get anywhere. It's impossible to do everything. You must learn how to let go if you want to know how to catch hold. On the other hand, you can't know what to focus on without the choice proliferation gives. Choosing from one segment can't be called a choice.

Chaos and the dialectical process have been associated in this book because they follow a complementary logic. Chaos starts off by putting the pieces in disorder. Dialectic ends up by putting the pieces together again in a different order from the initial one. As far as we can see from the cases we've observed, chaos is essential because it throws together pieces that will fit together later on. Then it's the dialectical process that fits these pieces together and establishes a new order of things where innovation is a complement, no longer a misfit. All this amounts to saying that chaos is necessary (provided it isn't destructive), but that innovations will still fail if there's no convergence, compromise and new construction to follow suit. The other conclusion you can draw is that it's good to choose an application and then keep to it. But if later analysis reveals that it isn't the right one, or is subject to certain constraints, then it's even better to agree to change course slightly. As the proverb says, "Better to bow than break".

This approach is entirely corroborated by the ideas Quinn (1986) proposes in an excellent article called "Innovation and corporate strategy: managed chaos". The author stresses the fact that initial discoveries tend to be very individualist and "serendipitous" (i.e. their end-result is never predicted in advance). Progress is chaotic and interactive and results are unpredictable right up to the last moment. He then goes on to speak, without actually naming it, of a form of dialectic when he says that the majority of the biggest mistakes observed in industry, like the Ford Edsel or IBM's FS system, had been overplanned and borne out on paper rather than developed interactively with direct feedback from customers.

And when we stress that chaos brings a renewal that we should exploit, we are echoing the ideas of de Noblet (1991): "It's impossible to manage the unpredictable and we must stop considering random events as disturbances that you can minimise in order to reach your goals, just by following predetermined plans or trajectories." This is taken up again by Cova, Mazet and Salle (1992): "Each time you do a project, this means you have random events to exploit, rather than random events to struggle with and squeeze into a predetermined strategy." This doesn't imply that you should "ride the bumps" and let events run your strategy for you. It means really exploiting random events, taking full advantage of them, so that you redefine your strategy better in relation to the changing environment.

Managing the Transitory State as an Investment

Project Marketing: Victim of an Unsatisfactory Relationship with Money

While we were describing the transitory state we saw some basic rules to help us get through it. There's one absolutely essential management rule to add to these. You must manage the transitory state as if it were an investment. What does this mean and why is it important to insist on this point?

Managing the transitory state as an investment implies that your expenditure during this time is money placed in the future. From a marketing point of view, the transitory state should be considered like an item on the balance sheet, not on the profit and loss account. This means that during the whole of the transitory phase money should be seen as financial relief for research, not as income to make some sort of profit margin, even if you do have customer funding. You can't calculate the true benefit of the operation in terms of real earnings. Its true benefits lie in this sum of knowledge that will enable you to make a product instead of a technical device. During this phase you not only learn to master the product but its transfer conditions to the customer as well. You likewise establish all the other elements involved in the transfer (i.e. price, service, payment conditions, distribution, storage, lead times).

If money does come in during this phase, it benefits the project in another way by giving it credibility inside the firm. These first earnings make a useful argument when faced with sceptics. It's a fact that the project is inherently liable to suspicion because it is still being run by Research and Development, and researchers are not supposed to have a clue about business. In contrast to what you can read about the NIH (Not Invented Here) syndrome, direct observation tends to show that people are suspicious of what's developed inside their own companies. On the strength of that, we really ought to be discussing the NNIH (Not Not Invented Here) syndrome. People don't believe in their companies' projects until the researchers actually come in with proof that someone outside the company is interested enough to put money in them.

So these initial earnings will encourage some people to think the project maybe isn't quite as ridiculous as it seems and deserves a closer look. In other words, contrary to popular opinion, it's not because a company believes in a project and puts money into it that the project succeeds. It's when a project succeeds that the company starts to take an interest in it and really invest, financially and otherwise. Until then it just allocates "wait and see" money. You can call this the logic of "external proof" (Figure 3.9).

It's true that researchers don't have much weight when they claim their product is the best and has the best performance. Nor can they manage to convince their company to give them moral and financial support. People only lend money to you when you're rich. Inside companies too.

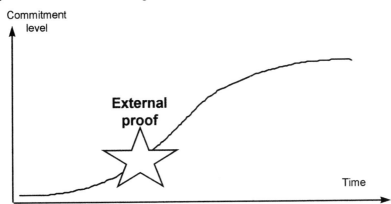

Figure 3.9 *Logic of "external proof"*

This investment concept is terribly important. Too many projects fall victim to their unsatisfactory relationship with money. They die out because company management considers the project doesn't bring cash in fast enough. The real truth is that they want to skip certain phases and make money too quickly with a product that hasn't finished its development. The product isn't even out of the transitory state yet and they already expect it to be a cash cow. Time is not the only factor either. There is also a question of procedure. It's a waste of time to try to speed up project launching. You do the work badly; you miss out stages in order to go faster. You give birth prematurely, but you already want the baby to walk.

Some American writers (e.g. Utterback *et al.*, 1991) have pointed out the potential dangers of going too quickly. Their warning is that it's harmful to hurry with some projects because you run the risk of short-cutting tasks like tests and guarantees or preparation of marketing programmes and equipment, for example. In addition, reducing development time when your project concerns an entirely new area will raise the costs without lessening uncertainty. The authors then present different project types to emphasize what kind of projects can be undermined by too much haste. Their classification is as shown in Table 3.1.

The writers say that in theory you can go fast in the situations designated in the table by 1, because they're familiar targets. The offensive is carried out by operational units and there has to be a very detailed study of customer needs and of distribution networks.

Table 3.1   *Speed of project development*

	Extensions of the firm's current market	New for the firm but established market applications	New, emerging market applications
Basic research leading to new core technology	4	2	3
Major enhancements of core technologies	1	2	2
Incremental change in technology	1	1	4

In cases designated by 2, you have to be prudent and develop product and market systematically and carefully from prototype development right through to testing and assessment. Speed isn't a success factor and large-scale development is counterproductive. The project can be run by an intermediary organization (called a "Greenhouse" by the authors): a sort of incubator. This intermediary has the job of carrying the project over to an operational division. With 3-type cases, developers need to experiment over a long period, learn and reduce uncertainty. The development has to be slow and sequenced with relatively low expenditure. This type of project usually takes between 10 and 15 years in Japan. Large-scale development is counterproductive in this case too. The situation should be managed by research until customer need has been identified. The product's usage value must be confirmed on a large variety of markets. The writers link this case with the very interesting concept of "market prototyping", which consists of ensuring that the product fits the market (and vice versa no doubt) by testing it with customers as early as possible and using their feedback for any further modifications (a procedure reminiscent of co-development). Cases classified under 4 are deemed rare, if not non-existent, by the authors.

If you consider that technological innovation as we defined it in Chapter 1 corresponds to what you see under 1 or 2, then you are coming to the same conclusions as the Americans. The diesel engine story is a marvellous illustration of what premature commercialization can lead to.

> The first commercial engine was delivered to a match factory. But four major problems that had been spotted during development and never solved soon turned up: 1) different parts broke at high temperatures and pressures; 2) the compression pump could block or burst because of the air compressor; 3) the wire-mesh nozzle clogged up and blocked very easily and needed constant cleaning; 4) lastly, the engine was particularly sensitive to the frequent and random changing of fuels, so there were big variations in output. So the Augsburg company was obliged to send two mechanics and then to call in Imanuel Lauster himself [Author's note: their most competent engineer in internal combustion] to supervise the engine day and night. It took a whole year of uninterrupted attention, and complete rebuilding of the engine, before it worked properly at last (Thomas, 1996).

You can imagine what this kind of mistake would cost today. The price of the operation alone would be exorbitant. But its failure would have such a negative impact on the reputation of the product that company survival would be in the balance. It would probably have cost Diesel a lot to co-develop efficiently, but he would have been able to share at least part of the expense with the customer. And above all he wouldn't have got into the very embarrassing situation of the supplier who imposes all the teething troubles on the client when he should have dealt with them prior to sale.

There are other more recent cases to illustrate haste-induced errors. For example, a fast-breeder reactor that was hardly out of the design phase when it was connected to the grid. To begin with, teething troubles meant it was only operational for intermittent periods. The reactor would start up, put on some power, then had to be stopped for technical reasons in view of the risk involved. It was never able to operate at a steady nominal capacity and was judged to be unproductive. However, this judgement was based on the performance and productivity criteria they usually apply to smooth-running, conventional-type nuclear power stations.

Several years later, after a series of mishaps, it was agreed to keep the fast-breeder on as a research facility for observation and experimentation. A Knowledge Acquisition Programme was started off on the site. It was to serve more purpose in the short run, helping researchers to master the use of fast-breeders on an industrial scale, than by producing electricity at prohibitive cost. A final decision was made in 1998 to close down the reactor on a permanent basis.

What happened there is relevant for innovative products in general. You can't make hasty judgements based on the performance criteria used for other off-the-shelf products. We tend to forget that standard products have been going for a long time and their teething troubles are over. Unlike the fast-breeder reactor, they are no longer in the investment phase. They have come out of the transitory state.

One fundamental point needs stressing. There has to be as much investment in the marketing function as the technical function. Companies visibly find it normal to invest in product development, and agree to do so. They also think it's normal to invest in capital equipment. But they stop short of sales investment. What do they say in their own defence? "We advertise and we do market surveys for our new product." Of course, but these expenses are treated as sales costs, as items on the profit and loss account and not on the balance sheet. They have to be offset by sales. It's not hard to see how difficult it is even for the biggest companies to spend £10 000 or £20 000 on a market study. But what's £10 000 if it can redress a project that has already cost you £1 000 000? That 1% may be all that's needed to save the thousands of pounds you would lose if you had to stop the project because your would-be product turned out to be a technical device.

But it isn't so much a question of the total amount at risk as of the budget you are going to take this money from if no budget has been planned for it. Will you get the £10 000 off operating costs, training costs, postage costs, telephone costs? You wouldn't come across this attitude so frequently if the £10 000 were really considered to be an investment. Where does the problem come from? It comes from the fact that, in any given year, someone will have to make an unplanned deduction from the year's budget. But, as the expense isn't forecast, they have to find a budget to deduct it from. So the £10 000 no longer corresponds to 1% of the cumulated budget for the project, but maybe 30% off the annual public relations budget or 30% off the annual budget for research centre communications. Understandably, the pill is hard to swallow. A department is asked to slice 30% off its operating budget, quite out of the blue, for something unconnected with it that would have gone unnoticed if somebody had initially thought of putting 1% of the project budget aside for a marketing study.

But a marketing study is only one commercial investment item. In his book on diversification, Rochet (1981) reports that 30% of the investments in successful diversification projects (and technological innovation launches are among these) are in fact marketing investments. Obviously, we are way off the mark with our 1% for the marketing study. Marketing investments shouldn't just concern the product. They should also concern the more technical part of the offer (price, lead times, service) and, more conventionally, sales and distribution networks and communications (i.e. targeted sales arguments and how to reach those targets).

Companies agree to invest in capital equipment and in

intellectual property to develop the product; concrete factors. But why do they neglect the rest of the offer? Why don't they invest in defining prices, service or sales techniques with as much care as they invest in defining the product? It all happens as if the idea of investing money on other items besides the product itself just did not exist within companies. Spending money fixing your prices, your offer, your sales techniques is not seen to be of any immediate value. Let's develop this idea on a certain number of points.

Investing in Price Definition

When companies have no reference available, no competitor product that does exactly the same job as theirs, their only way to price their product is to find out how much profit it brings to customers. How many industrial companies fix their prices by multiplying the cost price by 1.27 because their gross margin is 27% on their whole production?

This is sacrilege from a marketing standpoint because customers are excluded from the calculation. Of course, they may not buy the product if it's too expensive, but it's quite possible they will be ready to buy it for twice or three times as much, either because the product represents an insignificant fraction of its cost price or because this price also brings outstanding service.

Imagine a national power utility has a noise analyser which warns them a week ahead of time that the No. 5 bearing on their power generator is going to fail. A product like this would be beyond price for them because it could avoid major production stoppages at peak consumption periods.

There is only one way of finding out what benefit customers get from using your product. They have to be able to use it on a daily basis and you have to be able to see what they do with it, how they use it and what it saves them in time, material and personnel, as well as production, maintenance and control operations ...

There are more ways to have customers use your product than you would think. You can sell them something that foreshadows your future product at a symbolic price. It's of no importance whether this price is high or low, provided you tell them that it has nothing to do with final product price. What you are selling them is the chance to try out, to test and check. You're selling them a range of experiments to solve one of their problems.

You can also rent out your product. Or sell your services, doing the tests for them yourself in the form of demonstrations. But the ideal way to test the price is still co-development with customers. It means you both work together on a daily basis with the product, so you see the drawbacks and advantages for the clients straight away.

Whatever solution you choose, it's imperative not to leave the first customers to muddle through on their own. If they use the product badly, they will ruin all their chances of finding any advantage in it. Even if they do use it correctly, you are depriving yourself of the opportunity to weigh up customer benefit.

Whichever way you tackle it, this operation will take time. You may need to send one of your technicians or one of your engineers to the customers' on a full-time basis, and that costs money. But it's an investment. And if you think about it, it will cost you less to stay at the customers' and correct the errors right away than to suffer the dramatic consequences they often incur. If your customers have badly bonded the composite bicycle frames you sold them and now have to recall a whole batch of bicycles they have already sold to their customers, it will obviously cost you a lot. First, they won't want to hear another word about your product, so you can put a cross on all future sales there. Second, they will give you such a bad press that you'll have a hard time resurfacing.

Investing in Defining Your Offer and Your Sales Techniques

In addition to helpful price guidelines you can glean from regular close contact with customers, you will also be able to note what the customers appreciate on top of your actual product. Industrial clients never buy just a product; they buy the whole company.

While you are at the customers, you should therefore identify the type of training your customers' personnel need in order to use the new product correctly. You should note whether they're seeking to acquire technical knowledge from you that would enable them to evolve. You should also identify who's interested in your product at the customers, and why. This will help you spot the different motivations of personnel in their buying centre and choose the best person to deal with later. You'll find out that your surest ally at the customers will be someone who has a personal motive for being interested in your product. Such a person will always find a way of convincing people that your product is indispensable, even if it's very costly. Imagine that a quality manager has just been named by the managing director to instal quality in the company. You may be sure the quality manager will be interested in your noise analyser because it's a new system that will attract much attention within the firm. From the quality manager's viewpoint, it's irrefutable evidence to others (and especially the president) that quality management is being handled with energy and foresight.

People like this are your best sales representatives. But first you have to identify them and grasp their underlying motivation.

Keeping the Salesforce out of the Transitory State

Treating the transitory state as an investment implies that you don't put product promotion into the hands of your salesforce yet. To do so would be absolutely counterproductive and could jeopardize your project's future for several reasons.

During the transitory state, salespeople never have the same product to sell because there's so much product derivation at the beginning with different customers. Their sales arguments are outdated from one visit to the next because of product evolution. This makes a poor impression on customers and arouses the salespeople's enmity towards their own company because they don't like being taken for amateurs.

Besides, the sales personnel don't have many arguments since the product hasn't proved it's worth yet to customers. They don't know which quality to highlight and feel uneasy about selling. In other words, the company hasn't managed to sell its product to its salespeople. Yet they are the first customers it needs to convince.

What's more, sales personnel know the product isn't quite ready ("They played that game with me before; they won't catch me a second time"). Sales personnel are directly in the customers' line of fire and they don't like it. There are reasons for their lukewarm defence of the product. They don't believe in it themselves, so how could they convince customers?

Finally, when customers tell salespeople the product doesn't work or doesn't match their needs, the salespeople register customer complaints and transmit them to the designers. To begin with, this causes unnecessary delays, avoidable ones if the designers had initially gone with the product to the customers. Maybe the designers could have corrected the defect straight away since they have the competence to recognize and deal with the problem. Moreover, the product is their project, their baby. They want it to work, cost what may, so they have good motives for repairing it or modifying it as fast as possible.

Next, researchers are suspicious when salespeople either voluntarily or involuntarily give them negative customer feedback. "After all, did they really understand what the customers meant? Aren't they overdoing it a little, pulling down our product just because they don't know how to sell it? They haven't a clue. The product is fantastic, the best on the market." In no time at all, customer complaints are stifled. The researchers don't take in the criticism, because they don't take the brunt of it from the customers. This is essentially why it's counter-productive to give sales personnel the job of selling something that is still in a transitory state. Go about it like that and your product will never emerge. It will always be a technical device, a research laboratory toy.

Putting unfinished products into the hands of salespeople is also counterproductive for another reason. In fact salespeople have quite different motives from researchers. They are judged on their sales figures and on the profit margin they obtain per number of visits made or per number of products sold. Let's sum up the sales personnel's situation once again. They lack arguments and are still unfamiliar with the product, so they take longer to present it. And the time they waste on the innovation is lost time for the other products in the range, whereas these are the products they really know and know how to sell. Products that sell like hot cakes, too, when you need to catch up on points for your promotion. Meanwhile the innovation is a waste of their time, it fails to bring in money and it dissatisfies customers. Customers are most unwelcoming and technicians back at the office refuse to listen. Salespeople end up feeling like goalkeepers whose teams are playing very badly so they keep taking the brunt of all the other players' mistakes and being blamed for them too. It's very demotivating. The more demotivated they get, the less time they will spend on the new product, and the fewer they will sell. This usually ends by: "When you make me some good products, then I'll be able to sell them. But as for now I don't want to hear about your innovations again!"

This is advice for big companies but it's even more relevant for people setting up companies. It's essential not to hurry things by putting sales or distribution personnel onto the job too early. The product is not ready for launching if it is still evolving under customer influence. It continues to be in a transitory state and the best promoters for it there are researchers, who need to supervise its evolution regularly at the customers until a final definition has been reached. You don't try to sell your product during the transitory state. The task there is to optimize it.

Waiting before You Put Your Products on the Price List

There is no question either of publishing your product in the company catalogue before it's out of the transitory state. This is corroborated by what was said previously. It should only go on the company price list the day it's launched. This gives an official connotation to the product and concretizes its launching. Products only go in the catalogue when they have become standard products. But that isn't all. They can't be off-the-shelf products until the rest of the offer has been fixed, too. In other words, products should go along with specific prices and payment conditions, and suppliers ought to ensure they keep to specific delivery times. There is obviously a certain number of production problems and running problems that you need to solve beforehand.

Likewise you have to be able to provide all the follow-up services. None of this should be improvised at the last moment, when customers start to complain. Everything has to be planned, anticipated, right down to training the technicians in charge of future repairs and maintenance. And lastly, the salesforce has to undergo training, too, so it will be ready to promote the products efficiently.

Checklist

- There are three general rules in marketing that will help you to avoid typical pitfalls in technological innovation:
  - Let the project proliferate, and systematically try out as many likely and unlikely channels as possible to increase your potential field and choice range.
  - Get a complete picture of potential innovation markets and make segments, then, after careful diagnosis, rank the segments according to their accessibility.
  - Focus on from one to three market segments only, then devote your unrelinquishing efforts to the development of these segments until you've managed to put the product on the market.
- The proliferation phase may well be turbulent and chaotic but observation shows it's necessary for project success. From an empirical, non-intuitive viewpoint, projects that don't experience this turbulent, doubtful period are noticeably much more prone to failure than others.
- It's essential to have a collaborating partner, usually a customer, when you focus on a segment. This operation is called co-development. It enables you to share expenses. Above all, the customers' participation gives you better guidance in developing the product that's best fitted to their problems.
- Industrial customers are usually described by writers as being cautious, reserved people when it comes to anything that might disrupt or jeopardize what they do. Strictly speaking, this means they should reject all technological innovation (which is uncertain and disruptive by definition), but in fact not all customers do. Customer interest in innovation can be explained by their underlying motives and just how strong these motives are. Their motivation can be based on industrial or technical reasons or it can be commercial, competitive, financial, social, regulation-related, environmental or strategic. They can also be following trends. The strength of their motivation will depend on the comparative advantages or disadvantages they see in adopting the innovation, which is why a client with

everything to win and nothing to lose will accept the innovation more willingly than a client who has everything to lose by it and nothing to gain. Obviously, you find the pioneer customers – the potential co-developers – among the very motivated ones.

REFERENCES

Brown, J.S. (1991). Research that invents the corporation. *Harvard Business Review*, January.

Cova, B., Mazet, F and Salle, R. (1992). Le marketing des projets entre planification et laisser-faire. Communication of the 8th AFM Congress, Lyon, 14–15 May.

de Noblet, J. (1991). *Ruptures*, Art Press, Hors série No. 12, quoted by Cova *et al.*, *op. cit.*

Drucker, F. (1985). The discipline of innovation. *Harvard Business Review*, May–June, 67.

Jacques, J. (1990). *L'imprévu ou la science des objets trouvés*. Paris: Edition Odile Jacob.

Joule, R.-V. and Beauvois, J.-L. (1987). *Petit traité de manipulation à usage des honnêtes gens*. Grenoble: PUG.

Latour, B. (1992). *Aramis ou l'amour des techniques*. Paris: La Découverte.

Mangematin, V. (1993). Compétition technologique: les coulisses de la mise sur le marché. *Gérer et Comprendre*, June.

Millier, P. (1995). *Développer les marchés industriels, Principes de segmentation*. Paris: Dunod.

Nehme, C. (1992). *Stratégies commerciales et techniques internationales*. Paris: Les Editions d'Organisation.

Prokesch, S.E. (1993). Mastering chaos at the high-tech frontier: An interview with Silicon Graphic's Ed McCracken. *Harvard Business Review*, November–December.

Quinn, J.B. (1986). Innovation and corporate strategy: managed chaos. In *Technology in the Modern Corporation: A strategic perspective*, in co-ordination with Mel Horwitch, Oxford: Pergamon Press.

Rochet, C. (1981). *Diversification et redéploiement de l'entreprise*. Paris: Editions d'Organisation.

Thomas, D. (1996). Treize décisions pour un nouveau moteur. *Les Cahiers de Science et Vie*, Hors série No. 31: Spécial Rudolf Diesel, February, 46–61.

Utterback, J., Tuff, T., Meyer, M. and Richardson, L. (1991). When speeding concepts to market can be a mistake. MIT Industrial Liason Program Report, The International Center for Research on the Management of Technology, Working Paper 45–91, March.

Van de Ven, A., Angle, H.A. and Scott Poole, M. (1989). *Research on the Management of Innovation*. New York: Harper & Row.

Von Hippel, E. (1986). Lead users: a source of novel product concepts. *Management Science*, **32**, No. 7, 791–805, July.

Von Hippel, E. (1988a) *The Sources of Innovation*. New York: Oxford University Press.

Von Hippel, E. (1988b). Trading trade secrets. *Technology Review*, February–March.

4
Analysing Marketing Situations

In the previous chapter we saw we had to let projects proliferate and cover the widest possible field of applications before selecting target segments on which to focus. But there's an underlying difficulty to the apparently easy task of picking targets. You just can't afford to make random choices. There are two preliminary stages it's essential to go through prior to making your choice: segmentation and diagnosis.

By "segmentation" we mean describing the market as simply as possible while doing our best to emphasize its variety. This is achieved by using explanatory criteria (or descriptors) to classify homogenous groups of customers: the so-called market segments to which we're referring.

Diagnosis is the operation whereby you judge your own situation in relation to each market segment. This requires a host of assessment criteria to help you estimate the risk entailed by your company on each particular segment. Thereafter you can rank market segments in order of interest, and choose the targets. We now need to see how to carry out and exploit segmentation and diagnosis if we want to understand the way they work.

MARKET SEGMENTATION

Market segmentation means having a representative picture of the market, being able to visualize it. (These segmentation methods are developed further in Millier, 1995.) As technology is of prime importance when you're analysing the situation for innovative products, we will explicitly introduce a technical dimension into the segmentation here. The term "technical segmentation" will designate our operations to identify all potential applications for the new product: that is, the technical needs the product can meet.

But it doesn't just take unsolved technical problems to make markets, so we need to add a second dimension to the segmentation. In this case we'll talk of "behavioural segmentation", which designates what we do to spotlight groups of customers with similar attitudes to innovation.

Once you have obtained your technical and behavioural segmentation, you make a segmentation chart by intersecting them as in Table 4.1.

Table 4.1 *Segmentation chart*

	Application 1	Application 2	Application 3	Application 4
Behaviour 1		Segment 2		Segment 6
Behaviour 2	Segment 1		Segment 4	
Behaviour 3		Segment 3		
Behaviour 4			Segment 5	

In the table wherever the intersections between columns and rows have been filled in, they correspond to market segments: homogenous customer groups that can be of real strategic value to you. We can illustrate this with an example from the non-destructive ultrasonic laser project, where they pinpointed the two segments shown in Table 4.2.

What gives these two segments their internal homogeneity and what makes them different?

- In Segment 1 the customers work in a research laboratory with very proficient people who are utterly oblivious to price worries and spend their time trying to describe the shape of flaws inside composite parts.

Table 4.2   *Example of two market segments*

First segment	Second segment
British Aerospace shopfloor Dassault shopfloor Rover Group Laboratory	Vauxhall shopfloor Rover Group shopfloor

- In Segment 2 the customers want to instal the innovation on a production line with a high production rate, in order to locate defects in steel parts at a cost of less than 3p per measurement.

First, you will note that segment uniformity doesn't depend on the industry to which customers belong. So in fact there are aircraft companies and automotive companies in the first segment. On the other hand, automotive companies exist in both segments.

On the strength of this description of the segments you can see you won't be serving them the same way. You'll send your best technicians to meet the researchers from Segment 1 and offer them highly sophisticated, high-performance equipment. In contrast, you'll be sending a salesperson to see the buyers in Segment 2 to negotiate the sale of a fast, productive, reliable control system that operates at less than 3p per unit. From the marketing perspective, you can really say there are two market segments here.

Technical Segmentation

Technical segmentation begins by identifying what use the customers are going to make of your product. For instance, what we mean by "use" is:

- Products which are partly composed of the material you're developing
- Measurement, manufacturing, maintenance, calculation operations or others that customers will carry out with the machines or equipment you're developing.

Hence, potential uses for a non-destructive ultrasonic laser control system could be:

Controlling water pipelines in mountains
Controlling defects in metal blanks just out of the high-speed rolling mill
Controlling primary circuit pipes in nuclear power stations
Controlling fighter-plane wings in composite material
Controlling outdoor piping in refineries
Supervising cable-car cables while in operation
Controlling nuclear fuel quality
Controlling gas pipelines
Controlling rails already in place on rail tracks
Controls during development of fissile material
Controlling pipes in conventional fuel power stations.

Once you've compiled the list of uses, you need to use your intuition to subdivide it into smaller groups that each represent a specific type of technical problem. The intuitive approach works remarkably fast and efficiently in processing all the information collected beforehand either consciously (by enquiries conducted along specific interview guidelines, for instance) or unconsciously (by observing details that seem insignificant but ultimately reveal deep-seated problems). For instance, if you use your intuition to subdivide the applications list for the ultrasonic laser project, you might get the results shown in Table 4.3.

Of course, intuitive thinking can easily be discredited by people who retort that their own intuition is as valid as yours. So it's necessary to rationalize this initial step by carrying out three logical tests on the groups of applications. The first tests whether your applications and your list of functions are coherent. It comes in the form of a chart. This lists every function that's needed to meet the technical requirements common to all the applications.

Table 4.3   *Examples of applications for non-destructive laser control*

Applications	Defect detection in the field	Defect detection in fast-moving parts	Defect detection in hostile environment
Products	• Pressure pipelines in mountains • Gas pipelines • Pipes in power stations • Outdoor piping in refineries	• Metal blanks out of high-speed rolling mill • Rails already in place on rail tracks • Cable-car cables while in operation	• Primary circuit pipes in nuclear power stations • Nuclear fuel quality • Development of fissile material

This table is a valid test for your list: each application (or specific technical case) is met by a single innovative product that's defined according to its function. If the same product can be used for two applications, you must join up the applications and classify them as one. When the same solution applies to two cases, these cases can be considered identical.

The second test checks the coherence of your list in relation to competitor products. You need to construct a Technology/Application chart that includes techniques competing with your innovation. Then you show which technologies currently meet each application, or have the potential to do so. If by chance there are two identical competitor techniques for two different applications, you may find they are similar enough to join up (Table 4.4).

The third test consists of discovering and combining criteria (or descriptors) which can explain the differences between the various types of technical problem you have to handle. Pinning down these criteria is a valid testing process, because if you fail to justify these differences then you must go back to square one and redefine your applications all over again according to use.

When looking for criteria for your technical segmentation you should begin by describing:

Table 4.4   *Examples of applications for non-destructive laser control*

Applications / Uses / Functions	Defect detection in the field	Defect detection in fast-moving parts	Defect detection in hostile environment
	• Pressure pipelines in mountains • Gas pipelines • Pipes in power stations • Outdoor piping in refineries	• Metal blanks out of high-speed rolling mill • Rails already in place on rail tracks • Cable-car cables while in operation	• Primary circuit pipes in nuclear power stations • Nuclear fuel quality • Development of fissile material
Remote contact-free measurement		*	*
Instantaneous measurement		*	
Portable	*		
In-depth penetration of material			*

- The new product manufactured or new operation carried out
- Constraints regarding its use, implementation or manufacturing
- Its environment
- The problem you seek to overcome by switching technologies
- Problems encountered with competitor technology
- Functions customers demand, basic functions, functions competitor techniques fail to offer additional functions necessary to make the innovation fit customer needs.

Afterwards, you pinpoint everything in this description that can explain or justify the difference between one application and another or one group of applications and another. It's particularly important to root out criteria that explain the difference in terms of technical offer, in terms of implementation or of the technical problems the innovation has to solve. Once you find the criteria, you should work out which combination of these descriptors gives you the most complete picture of all the applications. Compiling a list of different types of criteria makes it easier to find your combination. For example, in the case of the non-destructive ultrasonic laser project, you could list criteria that concern respectively:

- Whether the material to be analysed is metal or composite
- Whether the equipment is portable or stationary
- Whether measurement data input is taken with
  - The parts for checking stationary in relation to the laser
  - The parts for checking and the laser in related movement
  - The parts for checking scanned by the laser beam
- Whether the task in hand is to detect, or to describe, defects.

You would get $2 \times 2 \times 3 \times 2 = 24$ combinations, if you were to do all possible ones. Not all combinations are productive here. We found six applications. The next step is to exclude all combinations with no apparent applicability in this particular field. You thus obtain the combination shown in Table 4.5.

Table 4.5   *Applications for non-destructive ultrasonic laser control*

Analysed material	METAL				COMPOSITES	
System configuration	Portable	Stationary			Stationary	
Measurement input mode	Static	Static	Relative motion	Scanning	Scanning	
Task required	Detection	Detection	Detection	Detection	Detection	Description
APPLICATIONS	Outdoor defect detection	Defect detection in hostile environment	Defect detection in parts in continuous motion	Defect detection in very large metal structure	Defect detection in composite material	Defect description in composite material

Behavioural Segmentation

The procedure for behavioural and technical segmentation is similar. You make a list of the customers you have met, then you use your intuition to narrow this down to clients who seem to have identical attitudes to the innovation or to show the same interest in it. This all depends on the impression they gave you. Their attitude may have been positive or negative. They may have shown various degrees of enthusiasm. Perhaps they seemed more worried about the technology than commercial aspects. It could have been the head of research who talked to you, or the marketing manager, the person in charge of environmental affairs, the head of the purchasing department... Each particular case bestows a different impression that you will try to give some sort of tangible form, by grouping together customers with comparable attitudes.

Next, you use three logical tests to give a rational basis to your intuitive classifications. The first tests the coherence of your grouping in relation to key commercial success factors. You then build a Key Commercial Success Factor/Behaviour chart. This contains two behaviourally different customer groups that each demand different success factors (Table 4.6).

The second test checks the coherence of your list as regards competition. With a Competitor/Behaviour chart, you should be

Table 4.6 *Chart of Key Commercial Success Factors/Behaviour*

	C 1	C 2	C 3	C 4
Price	*			*
Lead times	*	*	*	
Training		*	*	
Image		*		*

Table 4.7 *Competitor/Behaviour chart*

	C 1	C 2	C 3	C 4
HP	*			*
IBM	*	*	*	
DEC		*	*	
APPLE		*		*

able to show that two customer groups which work with different suppliers have different behaviour (Table 4.7). This backs up the previous test, since customers presumably choose the suppliers who bring them the success factors they're looking for.

The third test checks the accuracy of your behavioural segmentation. It consists of discovering and combining behavioural segmentation criteria that make it possible to explain behavioural differences between one group of customers and another. You go about finding descriptors for behavioural segmentation and for technical segmentation in the same way. First, you give a detailed description of the characteristic behaviour of each customer group and possible causes for these attitudes. Then you single out and keep only the criteria that best explain differences and resemblances between the types of behaviour.

Combining either behavioural or technical segmentation criteria requires exactly the same approach. You compile a list of descriptors of behaviour variables, but you only hang on to combinations that correspond with attitudes you have actually witnessed then compounded yourself intuitively.

In the non-destructive ultrasonic laser project, we identified three groups of customers with quite different attitudes:

- The first had so-called "research laboratory" behaviour because it was composed of scientists who were bent on increasing their knowledge and eager to acquire sophisticated high-performance equipment, however expensive and complex it was.
- The second group had so-called "production unit" behaviour: the customers here were a purchasing department, or a methods department. They compared the new product with what they already had from the point of view of cost and reliability in an industrial environment.
- The third group had so-called "maintenance" behaviour, the customers there being maintenance specialists who were going to choose material that simplified their job, made it shorter and less fastidious, even if it cost a little more than conventional equipment.

You can explain these three types of behaviour with the following criteria:

- Equipment-related motives: the group want to gain knowledge through the measurements, and increase productivity
- Motives related to problem location: online or offline.

If you single out relevant combinations only, the results are as shown in Table 4.8.

Table 4.8   Behavioural segmentation of non-destructive laser control market

Data acquisition	Offline	Laboratory
Increased productivity	Online	Production unit
	Offline	Servicing
Buying motivation	*Problem location*	*BEHAVIOUR*

The Segmentation Chart

The segmentation chart is obtained by intersecting technical and behavioural segmentation. You'll find market segments wherever the intersections between columns and rows have been filled in. We can illustrate this with a further example from the ultrasonic laser project (see Table 4.9).

Table 4.9   Segmentation chart of non-destructive laser control market

		Analysed material	METAL				COMPOSITES	
		System configuration	Portable	Stationary			Stationary	
		Measurement input mode	Static	Static	Relative motion	Scanning	Scanning	
		Task required	Detection	Detection	Detection	Detection	Detection	Description
		APPLICATIONS	Outdoor defect detection	Defect detection in hostile environment	Defect detection in parts in continuous motion	Defect detection in very large metal structures	Defect detection in composite material	Defect description in composite material
Data acquisition	Offline	Laboratory		S1		S6	S2	S8
Increased productivity	Online	Manufacturing unit			S4		S7	
	Offline	Servicing	S5	S3	S10			S9
Buying motivation	*Problem Location*	*BEHAVIOUR*						

Once the chart has been made, you name the segments. To do this, you need a complete list of the characteristics of the companies on each segment. Then you label each segment after the characteristics all these companies have in common. In this particular case, segments can be defined as follows:

S1: Control department for irradiated equipment
S2: Research laboratory for composites in cars
S3: Maintenance in the nuclear energy sector
S4: Control of long-length, continuous process products
S5: High-pressure pipeline control by field teams
S6: Measurement laboratory for nuclear energy sector and ship industry
S7: Control of composite part production
S8: Aeronautic research laboratory
S9: Modern fighter-plane maintenance
S10: Continuous safety control on long-length installations.

Naming the segments helps you to spot and locate customers, to make an initial approach and see how many clients there are.

The following list is an indication of the kind of descriptive criteria you can use:

- The size of the company
- What the company does
- The industrial sector it's in
- Where it's located
- Its production methods
- The department concerned (e.g. R&D, Methods)
- Where the company is in the value chain
- Its legal status.

In the case described below, for instance, you'll note that customer nationality didn't exert much influence on segmentation. There were English, French and German customers on the same segment.

However, this isn't always the case. When the market study was carried out on composites, European car manufacturers were all found to have practically identical requirements as far as research went on performance levels. From that point of view, technical segmentation was quite independent of customer nationality. On the other hand, their attitude towards the suppliers was radically different. English, French and Scandinavian constructors were fully prepared to go along with the innovators right to definition of the product, and subsequently to order it. German and Italian makers were more inclined to borrow the idea and have the product made by domestic suppliers.

Sifting through all this descriptive data makes you aware of one fundamental characteristic that's true of any approach to non-existent, emerging or turbulent markets: you can't quantify these markets until you have defined them. It's only through a qualitative definition of market segments that you can assess total volumes or income in each one, and quantify the market.

Using the Segmentation Chart

When you have built the segmentation chart, you will be able to:

- Define the offer to fit each segment. The offer is partly technical, partly non-technical
- Establish customer approach strategy by fixing inside targets and sales arguments
- Determine the range of products that fits all market segments.

Establishing the Technical Part of the Offer

Your initial step here is to specify what your product does by making a list of specifications of its functions. You should tailor your list to suit the definition you have of an application on a particular target segment. For example, the application for Segments 1 and 3 in Table 4.9 is defect detection in hostile environments. This application has already been clearly defined by technical segmentation criteria. Now these will provide the broad lines for product definition. Thus, in S1 and S3, your offer needs to be a permanent fixture that can detect defects in irradiated, stationary metal parts.

As we have already seen, making a Functions/Applications chart provides a good tool for drawing up product specifications. This chart is obtained by adding together all the use functions and functional constraints required to meet your client's technical needs. And since your Technology/Applications chart has already been built, you now have all the elements necessary to design a really competitive product.

Establishing the Non-technical Part of the Offer

You should set about establishing the non-technical part of the offer (e.g. price, service, lead times) and your sales tactics by using customer behaviour data. Price, service and lead times are determined on the strength of information gleaned from the Key Commercial Success Factor/Behaviour chart. For example, in S1, S2, S6, S8, customers will pay a high price for the product if there is a good technical service to help with implementation and with knowledge transfer on ultrasonic lasers.

Then you finish off by confirming your analysis with the Competitor/Behaviour chart. You can fine-tune your offer this way and be more than a match for your competitors.

Establishing Sales Techniques

Your sales techniques should consist of targeting one or more people within the customer company and then developing arguments specifically aimed for each. Behavioural segmentation is helpful here, too, because customers' behaviour is determined by the risks they perceive and by their personal motivation (see also Chapter 3). Since company motives are conveyed by the people in it, your inside target (the first person you decide to meet) will represent company motives for having your product. Take the example of a fully automated plant with mass production. If your high-speed machining centre means they only need one machine instead of three running parallel, you will go and see whoever is in charge of buying equipment.

It's not hard to devise arguments for each target and then elaborate them. You must consolidate your position by emphasizing everything that backs up customer motives and reduces what they see to be risks.

To sum up, specific, multidimensional definition of the segments helps you to plan sales action as shown in Figure 4.1.

Coordinating Your Range of Products

The work so far will help you plan your sales moves on a given market segment. When you have carried out similar work on all accessible market segments, you will be able to coordinate the

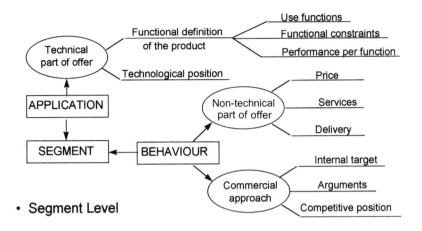

Figure 4.1 *Exploiting the segmentation twofold*

range of products you're going to offer, make a structured list of your activities and consolidate sales action over all the segments as a whole.

Segmentation centres on a core product or technology, and your range of products will stem from this. Each product in the range is made to specifications by fitting core products to customer needs and removing or masking superfluous functions.

We could coordinate the following range of products on the ultrasonic laser project:

- A detector of flaw characteristics: complex, sophisticated, hard to regulate, but sensitive and highly efficient in controlling composite material
- A detector of defects in parts as they move past online in harsh industrial environments (e.g. dust, heat vibrations)
- An onboard, travelling detector of defects in train rails
- A self-powered, field backpack detector for defects in high-pressure pipelines
- A detector of flaw characteristics for very large, thick, metal structures.

Updating Segmentation

Segmentation has a limited lifetime. It's only a snapshot of your situation in the marketplace. And the scene gradually changes. First, customers get used to the product. They have come to know it, master it, use it, buy it, weigh up its competitive value. Once the novelty has worn off, customer attitudes tend to alter. For example, this is why pioneer clients can eventually turn into demanding clients. Meanwhile, competition shifts and modifies segmentation. And lastly, you develop your product, so segmentation doesn't have quite the same relevance to your offer.

The segmentation will have changed its structure, but it may also have changed its basic shape. You could come across totally unexpected segments. For instance, new customers might contact you because they have learnt of your innovation through hearsay or from the press. New targets spring into place on their own. Then, of course, other segments will disappear because customers have deserted them to go onto another segment.

As it is, you need to update your segmentation often so that you always have the freshest information possible to act on. Basically, what you must do is resegment the market as soon as there is any important change in the marketplace or in the environment of your innovation.

DIAGNOSING THE MARKETING SITUATION

After segmenting your market, you need to judge your marketing perspectives in each segment, and thus diagnose the situation. (The diagnosis methods are developed in more detail in Millier, 1989.) Diagnosis is used to measure risk. It guides you in your choice of segments and in your attack strategy. There are two distinct parts to it: technical diagnosis (technical risk assessment) and commercial diagnosis (or commercial risk assessment).

Technical Diagnosis

Technical diagnosis consists of evaluating two different dimensions of risk: technology-related risk and risks related to the technological environment. When you want to evaluate technical risks, you use the following criteria:

1. Technology-related risk
    1.1 The technology's performance levels in relation to the application
    1.2 The technology's enhancement potential
    1.3 The technology's image
    1.4 The company's proficiency levels when using technology
    1.5 Coherence between project and company's technological strategy.
2. Risk related to the technological environment
    2.1 Supplier's capacity to keep up with your growth
    2.2 Risk of takeover
    2.3 Enhancement potential of competing technologies
    2.4 General demand for this technology
    2.5 Customer implementation.

Each of these criteria is assessed from 0 to 4 (or from − − to + +) by giving low marks to criteria that slow down product diffusion and high marks to criteria that promote it. You use the same method and scale to evaluate risk and uncertainty variables affecting the criteria. For instance, you're in an uncertain situation if you don't know what performance the customer wants yet. So you give a low mark to the performance criteria to avoid overestimating your position.

Once you have marked all the criteria, you calculate their general average then transfer the risk score to a diagram called a technical risk chart. However, you need to take precautions here as some criteria have more significance than others. These are called veto criteria because they stop you penetrating a segment if their score is low, whatever the marks are for the rest of the criteria. For example, very poor product performance is enough to cause failure. There's no point even in calculating the average because you know that maximum technology-related risk is involved (equal, therefore, to 1), whatever marks have been attributed to the other criteria.

When you have assessed both dimensions of technical risk, you deduce the value of your overall technical risk from that. You can schematize the situation as shown in Figure 4.2.

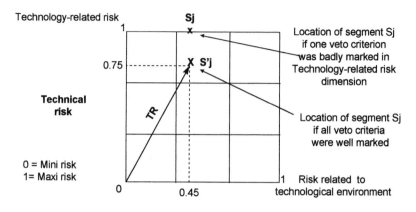

Figure 4.2 *Technical risk chart*

Commercial Diagnosis

Commercial diagnosis consists of assessing two dimensions of the risk involved:

- Company advantages and shortcomings
- Market appeal and constraints.

The following criteria are used to evaluate commercial risk:

1. Company advantages and shortcomings
   1.1 Experience and adaptability of the sales function
   1.2 Company adaptability
   1.3 Wealth
   1.4 Degree of synergy
   1.5 Business activities integrated downstream
   1.6 Service
   1.7 Company image
   1.8 Conformity with laws or regulations
2. Market appeal and constraints
   2.1 Market dynamics
   2.2 Growth rate
   2.3 Politico-economic risk
   2.4 Intensity of competition
   2.5 Customers seeking leading-edge technology
   2.6 Price-levels and returns on investment
   2.7 Size and volume of market
   2.8 Coherence between your strategy and the target market.

You assess commercial risk in the same way as technical risk, bearing in mind that veto criteria exist here, too, and you thus obtain the commercial risk chart (Figure 4.3).

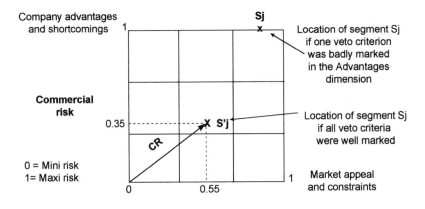

Figure 4.3 *Commercial risk chart*

Presenting the Results of Your Diagnosis

After assessing technical and commercial risk, you trace a strategic index chart. Your commercial risk index corresponds to the horizontal axis, your technical risk index to the vertical axis. Each segment is positioned accordingly on the chart, so you achieve an initial ranking for your segments. This operation is the basis for diagnosis. And there are recommendations to follow about how to continue exploiting the results (Figure 4.4).

Exploiting Diagnosis

Diagnosis gives you an initial idea of how to go about planning development, because it justifies the order in which you attack the segments. Your first approach tactics should be to launch your offensive on segments in the least risky zone of the strategic index (near the origin). But most of the time well-placed segments are soon dealt with. On the other hand, it isn't unusual to meet groups of market segments with a similar structure to the non-destructive ultrasonic laser segments. In Figure 4.5 you can

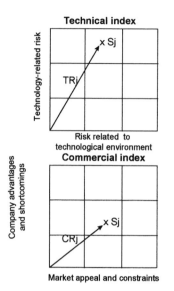

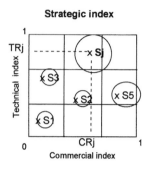

Figure 4.4 *Schematic summary of diagnosis*

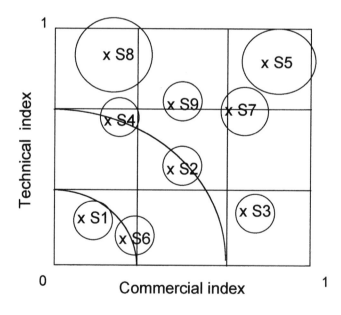

Figure 4.5 *Diagnosis of the non-destructive laser control situation*

see there are two small segments that are easily accessible in the short run without risk. On the other hand, segments with high stakes are very risky at the moment, that is, currently inaccessible. It would be suicidal to launch on one of these high-risk segments today without trying to improve your situation first.

If you identify the criteria responsible for such high technical or commercial risk this will give you guidance on what action to take and what strings to pull. Very often, just one veto criterion with a low score is enough to explain an apparently disastrous situation. Once these criteria have been identified, you need to ensure that it's economically and technically possible to reduce the risk entailed.

For example, on Segment 4, they still couldn't manage to carry out non-destructive control on parts in a fast-travelling linear movement, but they did know what type of research to undertake for that purpose and they were practically sure they would soon master the problem. So they did a simulation to map the positive impact of removing the veto, and found Segment 4 right in the middle of the most favourable zone for launching. This operation on product performance was momentous in itself as regards S4, because in fact the only reason for S4's poor position was the product's inadequate performance (Figure 4.6).

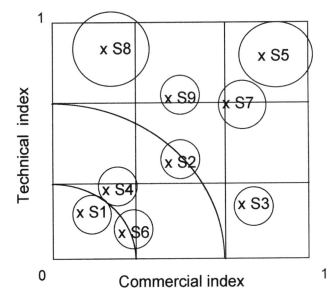

Figure 4.6   *Evolution of the non-destructive laser control situation*

Your strategy now is to review all the criteria that penalize your segments by assessing lead times in cost reduction and risk reduction for each case. Then you start developing a general plan of action in tune with your resources, priorities and collaborative potential (see Chapter 6). That is, you decide in what order you're going to penetrate segments and what obstacles need to be removed (i.e. what risks you must reduce on veto criteria) in order to do so.

Checklist

- People who don't know where they're going have little chance of reaching their goal. This is why it's essential to have as true a picture as possible of markets that are within your aim, and of how you're placed with regard to them. The two tools you need for visualizing the market and then mapping your situation on it are, respectively, segmentation and diagnosis. Segmentation helps you describe the market, with due regard to its diversity. Diagnosis helps you assess just where your company and your innovation stand in relation to each segment.
- Market segmentation consists of subdividing the market into groups with similar customer expectations and behaviour so that you can develop a specific marketing strategy for each segment. Segmentation has technical and behavioural entries for this reason. The applications are classified in the columns of the segmentation chart. This vertical classification establishes the technical part of the offer, that is, function-related specifications for the product or service which will fit the customers' technical needs. The horizontal classification in the rows of the segment chart is there to help classify customer behaviour and establish the non-technical part of the offer (price, services, lead times) and the sales techniques (inside targets, sales arguments, sales organization) needed to launch a successful offensive.
- To carry out market segmentation you take the following steps:
  - Use your intuition to segment the market from a technical

perspective, then rationalize what you find by identifying segmentation criteria: basically technical ones.
- Use your intuition to segment the market from a behavioural perspective, then rationalize what you find by identifying segmentation criteria: basically behavioural ones.
- Locate market segments in your segmentation chart, name them and quantify them.
- Update your segmentation as soon as there are any environmental changes.
- There are two parts to diagnosis: technical (technical risk assessment) and commercial (assessment of commercial risk). When you do technical diagnosis you use a list of assessment criteria for the technical risk involved. Likewise, diagnosing the commercial situation is carried out by means of a list of assessment criteria for the commercial risk entailed. Some criteria are more important than others. They're called veto criteria, meaning that when they have low marks they stop you penetrating a segment, whatever your score is with other criteria. For example, very poor product performance is enough to destroy your chances even if you have the competitive advantage price-wise.

REFERENCES

Millier, P. (1989). *Le marketing des produits high-tech, Outils d'analyse.* Paris: Les Editions d'Organisation.
Millier, P. (1995). *Développer les marchés industriels, Principes de segmentation.* Paris: Dunod.

5
Two Possible Development Strategies

Once through the transitory state and market analysis prior to choosing your segments, you're at last on the verge of launching your product and entering the market. All those preliminaries may have been necessary, but they're still not enough to guarantee success. Before you enter markets you have to take stock of their specific characteristics (what sort of competition they represent in particular) and know the features you want to promote on your innovation (e.g. it's the unique product to perform this function).

The object of this chapter is to present two alternative and complementary strategies that meet most marketing situations. We will call these:

- Niche or market-creation strategy
- Volume or substitution strategy.

TWO STRATEGIES FOR INVADING THE MARKET

As we shall see, there are two possible ways to ensure that your business is a commercial success. The first approach, called the niche strategy, is specific to technological innovation. You actually create markets by penetrating niches (or market gaps) where your innovation provides the only available answer to a particular need. A niche could be defined as a market that you manage to build barriers around to stop competitors infiltrating. But there's a point that needs stressing here. Contrary to general belief, these are not necessarily small markets. It would be truer to say that they're protected markets where you can work without any threat of competition.

The second method is more widespread than the first. The strategy here consists of taking over some of your competitors' ground and substituting your offer for theirs. We will refer to this as volume strategy, as most companies that choose this approach are out to achieve a quick increase in sales volume.

There is one essential difference between these two strategies. When you create your own market, your business grows at practically the same rate as the market and there isn't much competition. You could even say in this particular case that a little competition is better than none, because it gives some sort of reference point to customers. On the other hand, with a substitution strategy, your competitors are your big problem. The market is already in place and the only way to grow is to gain some of your established competitors' share, but they obviously won't give you an easy ride.

Your Relative Position *vis-à-vis* the Two Strategies

When you see these strategies in detail, they seem quite different. The fact is that you're obliged to exaggerate specific features, as with any classification, so you end up by rather caricaturing the situation. Exaggeration helps to clarify things, but, of course, they are never really as black or as white as all that.

You always have both strategies to a certain degree, but proportions vary. You can start by creating your market and then go on to invade someone else's segment. Using one of these strategies doesn't exclude using the other. They co-exist, follow on from each other or round each other off.

To assess your relative position, you can take the strategies to be the two poles of a dimension. This dimension extends from the most aggressive volume strategy to the most protective niche strategy. With volume strategy, you are looking for quick returns on investment through mass production, usually on heavy tooling: you "don't go in for subtleties". With a niche strategy, you are trying to promote specific technical features on a product you have developed.

As a general rule, this dimension is characterized by the three following criteria:

- Expected speed of investment returns. Companies with a volume strategy count on quick returns on investment. That is, they explicitly fix lead times and return rates on investments. In contrast, companies with a niche strategy are ready to make concessions on investment return times as long as their technology is being promoted in the meantime.
- Added value. This criterion is difficult to evaluate objectively, but, as a rule, added value of products or services increases as you go from a volume strategy towards a niche strategy.
- The relative importance of technical and commercial characteristics for product promotion purposes. With a volume strategy, the outstanding assets seem to be price, quality, lead times, service, the salesforce, ranking, distribution networks and advertising. With a niche strategy, it's a question of technical performance and the quality of collaboration between supplier and customer technicians.

This evolution can be schematized as in Figure 5.1.

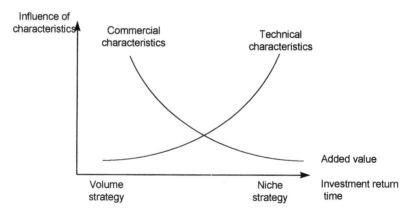

Figure 5.1   *Relative influence of technical and commercial characteristics*

The Runny Cheese

The "runny cheese" diagram is helpful in conveying the idea of a niche strategy in relation to a volume strategy and situating their relative positions clearly. Generally, a volume strategy means a substitution strategy for new entrants on existing markets. They intend to walk off with market shares that already belong to established technologies. A volume strategy can be visualized as in Figure 5.2.

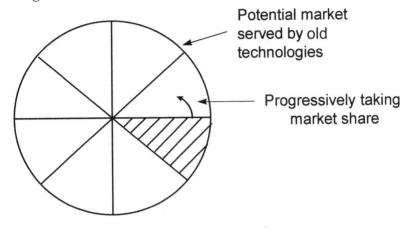

Potential market served by old technologies

Progressively taking market share

Figure 5.2 *Substitution market*

On the other hand, people use a niche strategy when they are setting up a specific market for their technological innovation. At first view, creating your own market can appear to be a projection of the imagination, something that's too good to be true. Yet MacKenna (1991) urges us to use this policy. He says that the real aim of marketing is to possess markets, not just to sell products, and that elegant marketing consists of defining your idea of the whole cake. This means rethinking your company, technology and products by defining what you can be leader in, because in marketing you possess what you're leader in. He goes on to say that by defining your own cake you won't have to make do with other people's cake crumbs, which you would if you were fighting for a share of the market. Leadership, he continues, is possession, and possessing a market can be a sort of self-endorsed spiral where you dominate. But he stresses that companies have to rethink definitions first and he cites the example of Convex, which defined a market between Cray (supercomputers) and Digital (minicomputers) before establishing its leadership on the mini-supercomputer markets.

It seems understandable enough that the concept of creating

markets should be alien to the majority of us. There's an excellent article by Green (1991) on creating markets for radically new products, where he says that most literature ignores the problem of how to start markets from scratch, apart from giving some naive quack formulas such as "demand can be identified from what people want". He gives supporting evidence in the general tendency to base strategic planning on unrealistic hypotheses, such as:

- Information on markets exists, is accurate and reliable
- Markets and competitors have been identified
- Offer/demand is a stable duo
- Rationality prevails in economics.

What Green basically says in the rest of his article is that creating markets is a matter of innovations making their markets.

This second, or market-creation approach, helps us to complete Figure 5.2 by "making the cheese run" (see Figure 5.3). This figure sums up the situation and enables us to see that both methods are feasible for promoting your innovation. But they can only be so if they're used in the right circumstances. So it will be just as legitimate to apply a volume strategy to substitution markets as it is to apply a niche strategy to specific market creation. But the danger (or the risk of being inefficient) lies in planning to attack a specific market with a volume

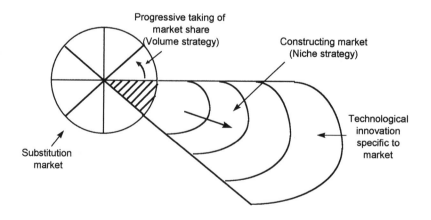

Figure 5.3 *The runny cheese*

strategy. Using a niche strategy on volume-orientated markets hardly seems plausible. The risk actually is that you won't convince the first customers to buy. You make them feel insecure because you take away their landmarks without providing others (and there's no market for new ways of looking at things).

Your strategy can also prove inefficient because target customers on volume-orientated markets are used to comparing offers. The problem is that innovations usually compare unfavourably with other products here, and you can't sell an offer that doesn't compare at a much higher price than competition. So when builders compare reinforcement fibre, an unknown factor, with the steel rods they have been using happily for 30 years, they still prefer the steel rods. On a short-term basis, they can only see the drawbacks of the fibre and the advantages of the steel rods.

Opportunities Vary

You will need to know exactly what the comparative risks are of choosing one or the other strategy. They both have their good points and their bad ones. As O.L. Barenton put it when he was thinking about establishing the ice-cream market in Europe: "This industry doesn't exist: that's the only case where you're sure of having some competitive advantage." He got this answer: "We're not interested in spreading our reputation abroad. You need customers to get profits and there aren't any customers. No one eats ice-cream in France. It's a refreshment for prohibitionist countries like America." Barenton replied: "It's precisely because there aren't any customers that it's good business. Wherever there are customers, there's competition. The need doesn't exist, but you just have to create it." They eventually came back with "Maybe that's a probability, but it's not a certainty". So Barenton said: "There's no certainty except the past. But we only work with the future" (see Detoeuf, 1989). Barenton's comments on ice-cream are very refreshing! Refreshing and very relevant to technological innovation.

Either you have no customers and no market, but there isn't any competition. That's a market-creation strategy. Or your market is well and truly there, reassuring but competitive. And that's a volume strategy.

As you might expect, nothing is fixed in advance with a market-creation strategy. There's plenty of room to manoeuvre but the prospects are very uncertain and indeterminate. On the other hand, with a substitution strategy, there are set rules and there's strong competition in place because the market already exists. You have to shoulder high risk levels, face the challenge of shifting well-established structures. So your manoeuvring room is minimal.

Of course, the ideal market would be a large, existing one, non-competitive, devoid of risk and growing strongly. But that's precisely where the myth of big, ready markets comes from. People want to have their cake and eat it too.

When innovators infiltrate new markets that are in the process of being set up, their strategy is somewhat akin to a chessplayer's strategy. At the beginning of the game, opponent players have exactly the same chessmen and an equally infinite variety of possible moves to try to win each other's territory. In a similar way, innovations have an exponential development (see Figure 2.1) and a range of possible moves at their disposal for building their markets and outstripping competitors. Right from the start of the chess match, players adopt a tendency (e.g. to attack or defend) which can be visible simply from their opening move. Likewise, an innovator's choice of first segments foreshadows a tendency (to a niche or a volume strategy).

Players continue to have a large degree of tactical freedom during the first stages of the game. However, they have already started to define their strategy by moving their pieces into positions that are protected by fellow chessmen. Each move in turn guarantees safe cover for a later move with another chessman. Sometimes players sacrifice small pieces so that bigger ones can advance faster and further. It's the relative value of the pieces that's borne in mind here. If you sacrifice large pieces early on, the chances are you will sorely miss them later on.

It's a similar case with innovators. Their safe progression implies attacking markets via small segments by developing products to fit customer needs and by building up references. Then they use their new assets to invade higher-risk markets and avoid wasting any initial time on "small fry". The fact is that it's not always easy to have a second try at segments you missed the first time.

Meanwhile, the pawns you sacrificed have enabled you to advance, and "clear the ground" for large-scale manœuvres, so that the invasion can continue with heavy armaments. But the chessmen are positioned in such a way now on the board that moves are becoming more and more restricted. Your strategy will be increasingly determined by the game and by your opponent's position, but also by the position of your own chessmen. Your current objective is to take the best advantage you can of a tight situation. There are still some moves possible, but scope is shrinking fast.

It's the same procedure for innovators who gradually leave the small segments they started on. These are no longer interesting, but they have provided valuable experience for future attacks on high-risk segments. Meanwhile, customers develop habits, competition takes root and there's less room for manœuvre. You can still act, but you have a reduced number of potential moves. As one industrial expert said: "You can innovate as much as you want in the packing industry, as long as the bottle is the same height, the same diameter and the same colour...!"

The situation is getting more and more like the one in Asimov's *Foundation* (1960), where he describes the path ahead as being traced out implacably with a series of comparable crises to face along the way. And, each time there's a crisis, the protagonist is completely divested of all freedom of action and only one possible solution remains.

As markets succumb little by little to the people who structure offer and shape demand, you realize increasingly that it's the game that sets the rules, and that fewer and fewer mistakes can be made safely. Henceforth, you need to hit your target the first time round.

It's always possible to win, whatever the initial choices are, but the more open the situation is to begin with, the freer you will be to act. Of course, it's your prerogative to take your innovation into a structured market. But in that case you will really need to find out the "one best way" and accept the risk of having only a single try.

Evolution of a Niche Strategy towards a Volume Strategy

Neither of the strategies presented above precludes the other. On the contrary, they can complete each other or evolve towards each other. For instance, a niche strategy can develop into a volume strategy, or vice versa.

Transiting from a niche strategy to a volume strategy could be compared to a sort of natural development process that all successful technological innovation projects follow, a process that gives rise to evolving, growing activity. A niche strategy is not a durable strategy. It's adapted for putting technological innovations on the market. It helps to identify and penetrate target markets that will take the new product further. But these initial target markets are never more than an intermediary goal for marketers. They are just stepping stones to larger, more risky markets that aren't reachable in the immediate future, because a foot wrong right now could be fatal.

If you use a niche strategy to launch your project, then your project will gradually shift, evolve, and grow sufficiently to be run according to a volume strategy. The marketing manager for the CVD project (a machine to manufacture electronic substrate) confided:

> Later on, we attacked the segments where you have the big Japanese firms who make silicon wafers. Obviously there were high stakes for us there because:
>
> - The market's large
> - The customers are financially sound
> - There's a large number of units needed
> - These customers are Japanese with very serious references
> - They have very strong investment capacity
> - They are loyal customers.

That's precisely the kind of evolution that Abernathy and Utterback recommend in a famous article called "Patterns of industrial innovations" (1978). According to them, you should keep on innovating until you find a product that satisfies the largest possible market. Once you have identified this market, you invest in a production tool. This tends to call a halt in product evolution, and from then on most improvements are made to the process itself, and aim at rationalizing it and lowering costs.

Initially it was a pilot unit in the research centre that carried out production in the reinforcement fibre project. Production went from two tons a year in 1985 to 80 tons a year in 1989. To begin with, the company concentrated on one application: renovating concrete pipes and drains. Then it shifted to industrial paving, which is a strongly growing, widely dispersed market. In 1990, the project reached industrial scale with a new production unit which enabled the firm to penetrate even bigger markets, like the manufacture of prefabricated concrete products or fibre concrete containers.

This case illustrates how a product that's still on the "high-range" market in the building and public works industry can have its production rates grow to reach substantial volumes. It isn't trying to compete with steel rods, and the volume produced is not quite up to volume strategy levels yet. But it tends that way, on markets the product itself created.

Evolution of a Volume Strategy towards a Niche Strategy

Evolution in this direction doesn't seem to make sense, yet it's fully justifiable. You come across it when innovators that have technology with a lot of potential applications are obliged to adopt a volume strategy at an early stage. They might have several reasons for making this decision:

- The firm has a volume culture. It knows how to run business on a large scale, not on a small scale.
- The technology in question necessitates use of large production tools (e.g. rolling-mills, chemical reactors).
- Markets have to reach a certain size threshold to become viable. For example, cellular telephone services aren't justifiable unless there's a large number of clients. What's more, initial investments are so heavy that you need to be able to count on big markets to offset them.

Research teams have no choice in this case but to do what they're told. However, it isn't always an easy decision to accept. There is much unused potential stored up behind some enforced choices. Project management teams often think their innovations are unworthy of a paltry fate like this. But although a volume strategy is considered to be a constraint here, or a necessary evil for starting up business and making references, it helps you towards independence and it means you have equities to reinvest in researching new applications, so that you can explore potential channels more thoroughly than before. And that's just how you go from a volume strategy to a niche strategy. In other words, the research team resigns itself for a time to applying the volume strategy laid down, in order be able to exert its energies on specific markets later on.

This type of situation usually evolves as follows. To begin with, there's a boost in production because of increasing sales on mass markets. This means production tools are being fully exploited; they are generating profit margins, covering fixed costs and making the business self-sufficient. Later on, part of that production will be withdrawn and set aside for conversion into other applications. These applications are to fit markets that are more demanding, technically speaking, where people are on the lookout for unique solutions to problems only specific innovations can solve. This is how you shift to a niche strategy: by penetrating markets that attach a higher value to your offer's potential.

The heat-transfer fluid project is a typical example of this situation. The project team had to saturate a production tool that was already in place, and resign themselves to invading the big chemical industry market where the company had references. But the researchers decided that their product's technical characteristics were being underexploited. So they went into partnership with an engineering consultancy to design installations and make maximum use of the product's technical features in the pharmaceutical and textile industries.

In a way, the single project split into two. One branch targeted the petrochemical industry, and followed a volume strategy. The other branch went to work on niches in the pharmaceutical and textile industries where customers demanded acute levels in technical performance. The process of going from a volume strategy to a niche strategy can be schematized as in Figure 5.4.

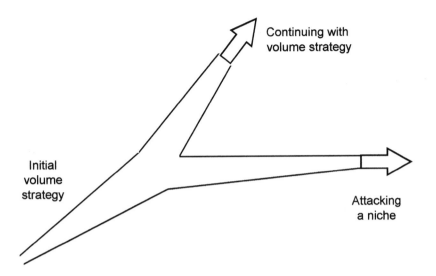

Continuing with
volume strategy

Initial
volume
strategy

Attacking
a niche

Figure 5.4 *Redeployment on a specific market*

A MARKET-CREATION STRATEGY OR A NICHE STRATEGY

General Characteristics of a Market-creation Strategy

There are seven distinct points that help to classify a market-creation strategy or a niche strategy.

1. With a niche strategy you invent a market which fits your technological innovation, that is, which appreciates the true value of your new product's properties, functions and performance levels. Meanwhile you try to overcome any technological or commercial obstacles that you have with customers.

Hamel and Prahalad (1992) emphasize the fact that "vocal command equipment, artificial bones, micro-robots ... don't just make the inconceivable conceivable. They also create a new field of competition. If companies can't manage to define a new competitive field, they end up high and dry on markets for traditional products that are already saturated." Creating your own markets means you automatically put yourself in a new competitive situation, one where you can exploit your advantages to the full.

The reinforcement fibre project gives a simple but very good illustration of market creation. Concrete reinforcement fibre did in fact create new markets, such as inside restoration of concrete pipes, the manufacture of armoured doors in lightweight, shock-resistant concrete, or of radioactive waste containers with a guaranteed life of 300 years.

2. When you seek to be unique, you need to spot potential new applications with technically orientated customers. Clients who are technically orientated are those who have had a tricky technical problem on their minds for some time and haven't been able to find a solution. They are more interested in technology and in answers than in "products", because they have already tried all the products on the market, but none has proved satisfactory. When you present technology to customers in this manner, it gives them the opportunity to tackle their problem in a radically new way.

A large provincial city was trying to find an economical method to renovate its main drainage system without having to tear up the roads and disrupt traffic. The city authorities banked all their hopes for a solution on reinforcement fibre, and were so motivated by the product's potential that they agreed to devote time and money to its development. You also come across technically orientated customers who buy innovations at their face value, without actually having any idea what the products can do. Glass or steel manufacturers who have organized their business around their furnaces become immune to the fact that furnaces are the biggest cog in their wheel as far as development goes. But if suppliers came along with a simple, versatile, economic way to make glass or steel, they could reveal this need and convert basically reticent people into technically orientated customers. "We discovered new applications for projecting concrete by keeping ourselves up to date on how building sites were evolving, and also thanks to the excellent collaboration of X [inside partners who were in charge of implementation]". An unquestionable advantage to this collaboration was the fact that the partners were building and public works contractors. Their expertise obviously helped the innovator, who was a metallurgist.

3. Projects using a niche strategy are usually run by research (or development) teams who are in contact with the customers' technical function. Innovators deal mostly with customer research centres, production departments and design offices. Technicians talk to technicians.

4. The procedure in a niche strategy is to open the project out to its technical environment, so that you facilitate its future insertion on the market. We will call this "technological marketing". There are three basic rules in technological marketing. The first consists of spotting applications that are addressed by the most similar technology to your own. This amounts to saying that you don't go looking for difficulty by attempting to launch your product on large, inaccessible markets. You go where your product fits real applications and where you can acquire your first references. The second rule is to spread out from this initial application, making maximum use all the while of the technical knowhow you amassed during your early experience. The third rule consists of weaving a sort of technical support web by going into partnership with research laboratories, technical centres, specialists...

When experts are closely involved in your project, this gives it sound technical support and credibility. And technical support webs provide good grounding for your product's future markets.

The company behind the reinforcement fibre project teamed up with the International (technical) Water Centre. The firm that developed non-destructive ultrasonic laser control collaborated with the National Steel Research Institute, with a laboratory specialized in the physics of materials and another laboratory specialized in the physics and metrology of oscillations (the LPMO).[1] The company behind the heat-transfer fluid project worked with an engineering office specialized in heat, an engineering consultancy, a laboratory belonging to the national nuclear energy authorities and a heat science laboratory. It also cosigned articles with university researchers.

Two examples can be given of the mesh effect in this technical support web. The first comes from the laser control project, and the second from the heat-transfer fluid project (see Figure 5.5).

5. With a niche strategy, you can't just follow markets and conform to them. Markets open because of you, and evolve because you stimulate customer reaction to your innovations.

---

[1] The LPMO is a team from the CNRS (French National Scientific Research Centre), specialized in the physics of frequency-based measurement.

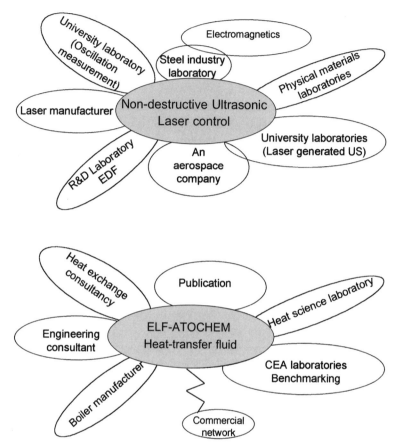

Figure 5.5   *Two examples of the mesh effect*

They are partly opened by the pressure of the offer. This is also called supply-side marketing, so in that sense a niche strategy involves a specific type of marketing. What innovators seem to sell are new ways of looking at things, radically different approaches to problems, rather than products or solutions. An entirely new vision of things could be:

- A new vision of production
- A new vision of dimensional control
- A new vision of machining
- A new vision of communication inside companies
- A new vision of the organic synthesising process
- A new vision of part design or assembly.

From an innovator's point of view, selling new visions of things means breaking old work habits, production habits, design habits, communication habits. Selling new visions means you may undermine traditional values on which customers have built their business. It means showing them there are other, unfamiliar ways of thinking things out which could improve their results. Selling new visions means that you assume customer problems in their entirety, while introducing a new set of values. For instance, it implies rethinking customer communication systems, communication flow and the consequences of intensified product flow. It also implies developing an adapted network, implanting this network and helping customers to exploit it... For example, renovation of drains or other concrete pipes could be carried out almost as easily as restoring a house-front thanks to the reinforcement fibre project. As a result of the heat-transfer fluid project, industrial installations could be heated at high temperatures without using overheated steam, which is dangerous and necessitates outsize security systems with strict and permanent leakage control.

Competing technologies were real "gas factories" compared to tubular membrane filtration. In fact customers usually had to go through a service company which picked up and treated the acid. As for the non-destructive ultrasonic laser project, it revolutionized non-stop defect control on moving parts.

High-speed machining centres are a very good example of an entirely new vision. The blueprints have undergone a metamorphosis here: the basic rules of traditional machining no longer apply. Everything is different: cutting speed, feed ratio, coolants, swarf removal, flow control, loading, noise, safety, the materials you machine. Customers have to learn from scratch all over again.

But you can't sell new visions – ideal visions for innovators – to all kinds of customers. They only sell to people who can identify with new ways of looking at things, people who are utterly confident in them. Customers that adhere almost unconditionally like this usually have a problem in a particular area of their business, can't quite put their finger on it, and are in search of something quite different because no adequate solution has ever been found. This helps to explain why, for example, a customer who is absolutely incompetent in computer science is capable of buying a local network without having the least idea of its potential.

6. With a niche strategy, innovators and marketers in general are obliged to bear part of the cost of market creation. It's important to realize that you don't automatically have an entrance ticket to markets just because there's no competition. There is a ticket, but it has nothing to do with competition.

7. Since there are no markets ready for you a niche strategy, you need to create the right conditions for applying your technology. It's what we call creating the right technical set-up. The right technical set-up for the membrane project was a specific filtration unit designed for the tubular membranes. And they created the right set-up for the reinforcement fibre project when they reintroduced a technique that involved piping the dry ingredients of the concrete to the projection area, before adding water.

The heat-transfer fluid project is an even better example. Until then, heat installations had been designed for traditional fluids like mineral oils and were adapted to their particular characteristics, limitations and weak points. The new heat-transfer fluid improved the overall performance levels of installations. But it was met by strong resistance because if you wanted to implement it you had to review your installation completely and commit yourself to a new, hence unknown, hence uncertain process.

So the company got expert help from an engineering office specialized in heat questions and a boiler manufacturer. They thought out new generations of heat installations to fit the fluid. They designed new thermodynamic loops to work specifically with it, and by it. For example, the fluid can go from $-10°C$ to $+150°C$ within a single loop; it stays liquid at ambient temperature and doesn't deteriorate.

Characteristics of Customer Behaviour in Niches

It's important to be aware that you can only use a market-creation strategy effectively on a very special kind of customer. But you won't have much difficulty finding partners for co-development among the so-called "technically orientated" clients.

Technically orientated customers are clients who are plagued with acute, recurring technical problems. The situation is so troublesome that they're looking for a solution at any price. They have already tried all the products on the market, but "they're all the same": "nothing works". This is why technology that seems to promise some radically new solution is likely to interest them more than a product that's just one more among many.

Potential clients here are usually proficient at their jobs and like discussing technology, so they're keen on the idea of collaborating with suppliers and ready to devote time, money, and expertise to help develop an adequate solution. In fact, this is their precise incentive for co-developing with suppliers. They are obviously clients who like meeting technicians and talking about technology. And they may even prefer techniques that aren't standardized yet, simply because standardized technology is tested, known and already outdated by more advanced techniques. Their main worry is to find the right technology for their needs, not to get the best bargain among competing offers. The technical function often overshadows the purchasing department at this point, because it's more competent at evaluating offers.

Customers of this type are usually thrilled to bits with your technology in quite an irrational way. They like it from the start, feel it's going to answer their needs. They intuitively have an overall, optimal view of problem/solution fit. But they don't reason it out; just use their intuition to guide them.

If you think about it, though, these customers have something more than an intuitive vision of the technology, because they have nothing to lose by it and all to gain, nothing to lose by relinquishing former solutions which were unsatisfactory anyway, all to gain by adopting a promising innovation. So they accept the teething troubles and implementation problems that will unfailingly come along with it. There are technical motives here and they are stronger than any risks which would be sufficient to baulk them. This kind of attitude helps to find all the good reasons for adopting an innovation.

What's in the Offer in a Niche Strategy

When you talk about offer in industry, you are referring to four elements (see Turnbull and Valla, 1986): product, service, price and lead times. But what you offer when you apply a niche strategy is quite different from a traditional offer. Each component is modified.

Product

The concept of technological solutions largely overshadows the concept of products here. Innovators offer package deals to customers, package deals of technical knowledge which they and the customers will try to fit to specific needs.

The company behind the tubular membrane filtration product knew more about electrodialysis than membranes. In the non-destructive laser control project, the company was better at generating ultrasonic waves by laser than operating a test bench. The company behind the reinforcement fibre project was more familiar with concrete composites than reinforcement fibre.

Service

The above factors influence offer, so service tends to be a large part of the deal on initial segments. Sometimes it's such a large part that it is in fact a service the innovators provide when they tackle problems with their new technology. In fact, what innovators initially provide is engineering and analysis of the technical problem in hand. They sell engineer hours. In the tubular membrane filtration project "contracts were signed with customer companies for systematic testing of their acids until they became sufficiently convinced of the equipment's utility and performance levels".

Innovators then perform a series of trial applications of their technology to the problem in hand. This is done with customer help. They go over the same things many times during this custom research phase and the product takes shape gradually after numerous improvements and reciprocal adjustments. It's worth noting in passing that customer participation in the search for a solution emphasizes the service side of the offer even more strongly.

There are unquestionable advantages for innovators in making substantial service deals. Once customers have agreed to test your new technology, service is an excellent excuse for keeping in with customers for as long as possible. From the commercial viewpoint, it reassures customers to feel the innovators are there with their proficiency and complicity, doing all they can to find a solution. It's also a fast and accurate way of identifying problems as soon as they occur so that you can correct them without delay. One step wrong at the beginning can compromise your project's future. Technical support shields you from clients making errors and then blaming your technology for them.

In the end, all these elements combine to give general satisfaction to the customers. It's as much to do with the quality of your mutual relationship as with any satisfaction they may have for technical reasons. And this satisfaction turns out to be essential if you want your innovation diffused on other segments, because what first users say is determining. It's a fact that less adventurous customers will readily trust first users' opinions, especially if they're negative.

Lastly, innovator services vary so much that they afford a good number of opportunities to differentiate your offer and put it out of comparison's reach. It's true that companies using a niche strategy try their hardest to escape comparison with competitor products, whether these products actually exist or are just in the offing. Even if industrialists admit that competition is helpful in opening markets (and when markets open it's a boon for everybody on the supply side), they still want their products to be incomparable. They argue "We already have enough problems adapting our technology just to avoid wasting our energy fighting competition".

Price

Companies with a niche strategy are more touchy about price than they are about any other part of the offer. They never quite know what price levels to fix, and hesitate between two extremes:

● High prices, which generate money, put the product out of reach of comparison, but harness you to market segments where price isn't a very important factor

- Low prices, which foreshadow your future ambition to penetrate big markets, but delay absorption of research costs.

Service has definite advantages price-wise. When your offer includes a large number of services, you can disguise product price behind all the service charges in your bundle. That way, the price of the innovation itself isn't so obvious: you are not just selling a product at a given price. This will help you to postpone price-fixing as long as possible and have more leisure to assess your innovation's real worth to customers. Strictly speaking, customers who want a solution "at any cost" care little about price because their strategy is also an investment strategy like yours.

You never meet given products at given prices on the first segments of technically orientated markets because it's very hard to make accurate prior evaluations of what innovations are worth to customers. Price-fixing is never calculated objectively anyway, as no one is quite clear about what elements to include in the calculation. It's true, among other things, that you need to have an idea of the quantities sold when you calculate prices if you want to determine returns on your investment.

With a niche strategy, there's no justification for making a certain number of clients bear the brunt of your investment costs, because research investment is usually very expensive. All the projects we observed that used a niche strategy had already spent between four and ten years researching before the companies decided to go ahead and make money out of that research. On the other hand, it's quite impossible to base price on the cost of materials: it would be senseless, even degrading, to sell a technological innovation for a song when it brings a new solution after years of research.

So in general the markups are high compared to the price of competing products, (£1000 for a kilo of aluminium alloy as a substitute for standard aluminium, for instance). One of the advantages of markups like this is to filter demand, so that companies can keep up an adequate output in spite of limited laboratory production facilities. Charging high prices also has a positive psychological effect on company members, as we have already said. As soon as thousands of pounds start rolling in, your project becomes credible. What's more, these initial thousands make your business a little more self-sufficient: it is now partly self-funding (or you get the impression it is). Whatever the case may be, the markups here are calculated to cover at least the direct costs (that is: materials, time, energy), excluding intellectual investments and excluding depreciation.

On the other hand, companies agree that markups could be a handicap when you are targeting mass markets, which are more price-sensitive and more competitive. This is what happened with the reinforcement fibre project. The fibre's sales price was around ten times the cost of materials, which did away with any chances the fibre might have had on mass markets.

Lead Times

The concept of delivery or supply lead times is irrelevant as far as niches go, because innovators don't deliver on a recurring basis. At most, you could talk about availability lead times for prototypes, implementation lead times, lead times for reaching $X\%$ of the nominal capacity, or development lead times. As it is, lead times are not usually the chief preoccupation of customers who want to buy the sort of products that sell in niches.

Marketing Resources Deployed in a Niche Strategy

The so-called "marketing resources" you need to have at your disposal are communications, information, planning, organization and people (for a full discussion on potential marketing strategy aids see Turnbull and Valla, 1986). With a niche strategy, these resources haven't been developed to any extent because the marketing side is not very structured yet. But they do exist, and their characteristics are as follows.

Human Resources

The main people in projects are technicians working on the development. They are in contact with the customers' technical function to co-define and co-develop the product.

Sales Organization

This doesn't need to be very structured. On the contrary, it must be as flexible and reactive as possible. Generally, it comprises R&D teams who ensure the marketing function by interfacing with customers.

Information

It would be quite inconceivable to have a highly developed sales information system in a niche strategy. Information here is technically orientated, which seems logical when your primary objective is to define and develop a product. Nevertheless, as we saw in Chapter 3, you are still going to base your choice of segments on information you glean from the marketplace. So, even if you are following a niche strategy, one market study at least is a prerequisite (one like that described in Chapter 4, for instance) when you intend to develop your product.

Planning

Planning should be neither too formal, nor too rigid, nor too detailed because that could impede the gradual convergence of offer and need. Development plans can be worked out little by little in the natural course of events, according to the opportunities that arise and technical knowledge acquired. However, it's essential to indicate what successive segments you're going to focus on and at what stage you intend to commercialize your product.

Communications

Communications tend to be discrete with a niche strategy. There are two commonly used methods: scientific-type communications (scientific publications and congresses) and participation in specialized exhibitions. The aim of scientific communications is to give yourself a name, a landmark in time and credibility through your joint publications with scientific laboratories. (The heat-transfer fluid project, for example, issued a joint publication with a heat research laboratory.) When you participate in exhibitions and business fairs, your main aim is to make your innovation known and to test customer attitudes. It's a way of measuring market temperature and catching hold of the first people who spontaneously show some interest. Communications of this kind also function interactively: they're an opportunity to test the reactions of people present, of your readers too, a foretaste of the sort of welcome your innovation can expect on the market, and its future position there.

People from the company behind the electronic substrate (CVD) project attended scientific seminars to see their product's impact on potential clients. One of them commented "Their curiosity is aroused as soon as the concept is presented, and they immediately start looking for solutions or would-be applications".

However, if you intend to communicate in niches you should pick specific targets in small numbers so that you can manage to visit them all later. As Abratt (1986) points out, communication on paper helps to stir interest but it never makes people buy. A niche strategy has to be relayed through face-to-face meetings where customers can discuss the technology.

Whatever the case, communications need to be discrete: customer expectations mustn't be raised above a feasible level. In fact, ostentatious advertising is often counterproductive both outside and inside companies, because people tend to think it's exaggerated. So it's advisable to show discretion until you're really confident, the danger being that initial feedback could be unfavourable just when you happen to be in the spotlight.

A SHARE TAKEOVER STRATEGY OR A VOLUME STRATEGY

General Characteristics of a Volume Strategy

A volume strategy can be characterized as follows:

1. It consists of going for mass markets straight away. The people who use it are often driven by the need to saturate a specific production tool or to spread the onus of heavier fixed costs as fast as possible. There are no concessions in this

particular case: "either you use 80% of your capacity or you shut down."

2. The surest way to find mass markets quickly is to head straight at large existing ones. If you do attack like this, your innovation will obviously become a substitute for existing products in the eyes of purchase-orientated customers. By "purchase-orientated" customers, we mean people who are already satisfied with existing solutions, people who have elaborated their own specific criteria on which to base any comparisons between new products and the ones they use. The most striking example of this situation is the battery-separator project, because it provided a substitute for cellulose in batteries. The measurement computer project provided a substitute for a computer, in the form of a dedicated machine. The heat-transfer fluid project developed a substitute for mineral oils. And the project for composites came up with a substitute for traditional materials in a widely distributed sports article.

3. These kinds of products are generally managed by marketing functions or sales functions which interface with customers' purchasing departments.

4. A volume strategy consists of taking over market shares swiftly and surely. This is why you should base your attack on strict, hard-line marketing tactics. That implies a lot of rigour when you collect data, when you plan out your strategy, and when you put it into action. In other words, you need to be thoroughly familiar with the market and its segmentation and know how competition is placed on each of these segments as well. The next step is to launch an offensive on areas where you are most likely to have a competitive advantage. A justifiable approach, because competition is seen as a hindrance on volume-orientated markets. This is why the situation is usually unfavourable for new entrants who have to prove immediately that they can do it better or more cheaply without disrupting the market. Innovators need to be careful to give customers exactly what they want, basically by ensuring that there's continuity of materials and manufacturing processes. The battery-separator project illustrates this kind of situation. The innovators couldn't substitute the glass wool for cellulose. They were forced to use a blend, to avoid problems

with manufacturing and costs. Innovators cannot afford to make mistakes here. They have to play the right card from the start, analyse the situation very accurately and get a clear grasp of the market's dynamics, segmentation and structure. They also need detailed knowledge of the sector, of customer behaviour and expectations, of their competitors and how they stand in comparison, and of the power politics that prevail. Your success in volume-orientated markets depends on this because these markets are already structured and there isn't much room to move. Decision making is extremely limited. You can't afford to go wrong. In fact, how innovators proceed in volume-orientated markets depends far more on who, or what, is where than it does in niches. Perfect knowledge of the markets is therefore a must, since innovators are very cramped by competitors and customers, competitors who end up standardizing their products, and customers who are geared to those competitor products.

Sometimes there's only one solution in this context. And you must find it. The battery-separator project is an exemplary case. Strong competition was already well rooted in the market so the innovators had hardly any potential openings. But they made a meticulous, painstaking analysis of the sector and the various interests in play among the people there. And they managed to find the right crack to squeeze their way in.

First you analyse the situation, taking care to segment the markets as rigorously as possible. Then you draw up a plan of action which you apply carefully and systematically to avoid omitting any important factors. You have to see that your strategy is very strictly defined, likewise the way you carry it out.

Basically what you need to do before you start making inroads into a difficult, crowded market is to prepare the essentials for your expedition, get all the right equipment, train well and be inwardly ready for quite a few problems. You mustn't forget the dangers, but the main thing is to steer straight and keep to a set strategy.

There is one particular case that's favourable to new entrants in volume-orientated markets. It occurs when innovators destroy a monopoly that competitors have been inflicting on customers for years, to the point of seriously annoying them. That was precisely what happened with Rhône-Poulenc's fibre, Kermel, which challenged the monopoly created by Dupont de Nemours' fibre, Nomex, to the general satisfaction of the customers.

5. Any sales investments you have to make with a volume strategy consist essentially of the costs incurred when you take over market shares. What you're paying is the price of your fight with competition. Few figures have been published on these costs, though Davidow (1986) suggests that if you want to forge yourself an honourable position in a leader-held market then your sales investments have to be equivalent to 70% of that leader's income. Which is a good reason for trying your hand at quite small or scattered markets first, before you take on IBM at computers.

6. Existing markets reassure, because "you know where you're going". The customers are there, so you're sure of finding them. On the other hand, they have already got used to buying different technology or competitor products and have been satisfied with these for a long time now. This is why, unlike technically orientated clients with their specific motives, customers orientated by industrial purchasing will dismiss, reject and refuse products according to their perception of the risk involved. As this would indicate, innovators tend to penetrate markets where they aren't rejected rather than markets where they are actually accepted. This is quite the opposite of a niche strategy, where you seek to be incomparable. In fact, in volume-orientated markets, you come face to face with technologies or competing products that clients automatically compare with your innovation. The only answer is to use the same weapons as your competitors and try to improve your relative position. In the battery-separator project, clients compared the price, absorbency and mechanical resistance levels of the glass wool with the same characteristics in cellulose. In the heat-transfer fluid project, they compared the price, heat capacity and heat resistance of the new product to the same characteristics in mineral oils.

At first sight, you could argue that a volume strategy seems to contradict two main theories in technological innovation marketing: the myth of large, existing markets and market construction. Can we really say, in that light, that a volume strategy is part of technological innovation marketing? A more in-depth analysis indicates it is. In fact, even if it's true that potential customers already exist in volume-orientated markets, companies always take advantage of market diversity to choose segments they are sure they can penetrate. And these segments are not the ones with the biggest volume. In fact, a market already existed for the battery-separator project: the car-battery market. But the innovators had gone into partnership with a firm that had only a 5% share in that market, so their access was limited to this small segment during the launch period. Added to this, glass wool constituted only 30% of the partner's product because the suppliers had to respect a certain continuity in materials. This reduced their market share to 1.5%. However, it gave them a foothold in the automotive industry. The generic market did exist already but the glass wool market within that was very uncertain. It had to be built up through the partner in a similar way to a niche strategy. The difference is that the partner wasn't a customer.

Characteristics of Customers in Volume-orientated Markets

We saw previously that typical customers in niches were technically orientated. You find another specificity with the customers you meet in volume-orientated markets. They are industrial-purchase orientated. Unlike technically orientated customers, they're fully satisfied with existing products that address their needs, so they don't feel any urgency about buying an improved version, especially when the improvement doesn't concern them. On the other hand, their usually smooth-running business and manufacture will definitely feel the adverse ripple effect of your innovation. In short, purchase-orientated customers can only see advantages to keeping their old product and drawbacks to adopting new ones, because they are acutely conscious of risk (technical, financial, service-related risks, risks concerning their relationship with you, risks related to lead times). In fact, their "objectivity" will drive them to analyse and measure the risks they think they would entail by adopting your innovation. And that clouds the picture. Everything clubs together to make their analysis dissuasive rather than persuasive, because they have a biased list of all the good reasons they can think of for not buying.

You shouldn't expect much help from this type of client. It's usually the purchasing department that deals with visiting suppliers. And purchasing departments work according to procedures, formal evaluation grids which filter all new suppliers and all new products. This is why we call them purchase-orientated clients. And the process is repetitive, algorithmic, analytical, systematic... Nothing is left out.

Here, then, technological innovation is subject to the same rules as all the other products. It has to work from the word go and it shouldn't disrupt continuity in the use of materials or in the process − or affect the clients adversely in any way. It also needs to satisfy quality levels that customers impose and measure themselves with instruments and procedures that were custom-built to work with what they used before. So old products have a good headstart.

It's an easy guess to make that purchase-orientated customers won't be spontaneously interested in co-development, because they won't necessarily see any immediate value in it. This makes the innovators' task even harder than in niches, but that doesn't mean it's impossible. If you explore a little, you practically always find a purchase-orientated customer with sufficient motivation to take an interest in your project. This client will play a pioneer role, and collaboration will be your key to the market. You can be guided in identifying customer motivation by the list suggested in Chapter 3. Table 5.1 summarizes behavioural differences between these two types of client.

There is nothing particularly novel about the characteristics attributed to purchase-orientated customers: they are directly inspired by the behavioural characteristics generally published on industrial customers. But their originality stems from the fact that we have only linked these characteristics to purchase-orientated clients here, thus distinguishing them from technically orientated customers. The most obvious lesson from this is that it's wiser to apply a volume strategy as if clients were people who needed convincing and reassuring, than as if they were inherently on your side. You might avoid some nasty surprises that way.

Finally, you have to be aware that clients are never entirely

Table 5.1   *Comparison of technically orientated and industrial purchase-orientated clients*

Technically orientated clients	Industrial purchase-orientated clients
Cup half-full	Cup half-empty
Right brain	Left brain
Sees advantage first	Sees drawbacks first
Reference to positive aspects	Automatic initial rejection
Intuitive adoption	Bargaining
Technological approach to problem	Economic approach
Technical motivations	Socio-economic motivations
(research on unique solution)	(money, regulation)
Adoption decision	Buying decision
Global and systemic vision	Analytical vision (slicing salami)
Nothing to lose and everything to gain	A lot to lose and not much to gain

technically orientated or entirely purchase-orientated towards any particular product. They may behave like technically orientated customers until their technical problem has been adequately addressed, then become purchase-orientated after they have been receiving the same supplies regularly for some time.

Likewise, car manufacturers can have both attitudes. It depends what part of their business is affected by the innovation. Salle and Silvestre (1992) inform us that the closer an event is to a company's main activity, the higher the stakes are but the more disastrous failure can be as well. What the authors mean by "main activity" is no less than the following:

Supply (input) → Production (process) → Sales (output)

For example, the larger automotive companies will probably be industrial purchase-orientated to avoid any risks when they introduce innovations on production lines or assembly lines. They obviously couldn't put up with stoppages on the assembly line, or the necessity for recalling 10 000 vehicles to the factory because defective safety systems had been mounted. Suffice to remember the dramatic story of a pleasure-boat builder called Bénéteau who had to recall hundreds of boats at his own expense and repaint them, because their original coat of special anti-algae paint started to flake off after a few months at sea. It's easy to imagine how scrupulously the boat builder will be sounding out new paints that suppliers bring along in the future.

On the other hand, parallel to this, it's quite conceivable for the same car companies to be technically orientated towards any solutions that could solve safety and design problems on improvements or modifications to their vehicles. This is why accessories like air bags, ABS and "green tyres" have established a place, regardless of price and regardless of the legendary claim that only price counts in the automotive industry.

What's in the Offer in a Volume Strategy

With a niche strategy the emphasis goes on defining the technical part of the offer (product, solution, implementation), whereas with a volume strategy the non-technical side is much more important. Price and terms of sale are a new source of worry here. The range of services that you're going to offer with your innovation has to be elaborated, too: aftersales service, training, installation, preparations for use, the trial period, help with implementation... At this point, you mustn't forget to incorporate all possible services that the customers decide they need once they have tested your product.

The company behind the heat-transfer fluid project had to organize a complete recovery service for its product. The fluid was supposed to be regenerated after a certain amount of usage. It could on no account be thrown out at random, since it was a pollutant. The company likewise had to implement a customized heat-calculation service prior to sales to advise customers on the most appropriate overall solution with their fluid.

As we have had the opportunity to see, the service side to niche offers is proportionately higher in early deals than it is later on. So you can make a point of selling services to the first customers. For example, this could be feasibility studies on the innovation, or a series of tests or trials on it, at a certain charge. With hindsight, you realize this system has some advantages. First, it implicates customers without actually obliging them to make large, chancy investments in industrial equipment. It also represents some guarantee of customer motivation, because people don't go in for this kind of operation without thinking twice. In fact it's quite an elegant way to shunt off time-wasting dilettantes. Second, it does away with free, random tests that tend to multiply, cost a lot in demonstration material or time and soon use up all the production capacity on small facilities. The worst case is when you completely paralyse your pilot unit on a semi-permanent basis just to make free samples for a big customer who performs lethal tests on them and gives no information in return. You don't know what the samples are used for, which means most of the benefit of the operation goes to the wind. No one checks whether the product is correctly used. No one checks whether there is an adequate system to measure the product's characteristics when it's in operation. No one knows what the product's real application is. And, in the meantime, the pilot unit is barred from more lucrative operations, and from pursuing the development operations for which it was originally planned.

Competition is so tough in volume-orientated markets that innovators have to ensure their offer is comparable by adjusting it to competitor products. Sometimes they may have to screen, disguise or actually sacrifice some of the characteristics or performance levels of their innovation. Sacrifice is not too strong a word: innovators sometimes feel as if their brainchild was being decapitated. Anyway, it appears to be useless, even harmful, to offer customers more than is necessary.

Here is an example from the heat-transfer fluid project. This fluid has a far greater range of usable heat properties than its organic counterpart. Yet the company had to align these properties with mineral oil characteristics to be competitive in the market. So now, as customers see it, this fluid is within the norms. They don't realize that it goes far beyond them.

Figure 5.6 illustrates the principle of adapted response and superfluous response. It's a good idea to meet clients' demands, performance-wise and function-wise, with something that's equivalent or only slightly better. On the other hand, it's useless to offer performance levels and functions that far exceed customer needs. Your offer should be "just what's necessary". If you don't respect this basic rule, you may find your strategy counterproductive in more ways than one. To begin with, customers can get the impression they're paying for performance levels or functions they don't use. Next, they will be tempted to judge the innovation harshly because it serves them no purpose. Making oversize offers can be an unnecessary form of self-punishment.

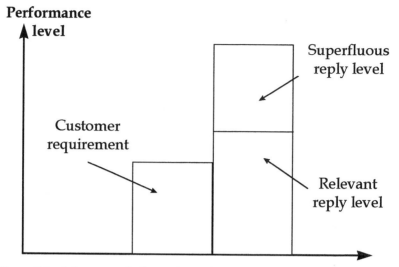

Figure 5.6   *Adjustment of offer to demand*

Marketing Resources Deployed in a Volume Strategy

Salesforce

The period prior to selling corresponds to a phase in the project when the company tries to find salespeople, then sets about training them. "Training is essentially about the marketing objectives being pursued, technical information (knowledge of the product), competition (knowledge of competitors, competitive advantages and disadvantages of the product) and sales arguments to develop." Sales arguments should be based on four or five strong points at the most. They should include detailed characteristics of competitor products so that salespeople also have counter-arguments at their disposal.

This is all very well, but training can never replace experience in the field. Real training comes gradually from listening to customers: this is how salespeople perfect their arguments and improve their performance (Figure 5.7). It's a simple fact that partly explains why sales often plummet after a good start.

This good start can be explained by initial sales to lead users, and sometimes to curious competitors. Then sales begin to drop after a certain time. How long this is depends on how long

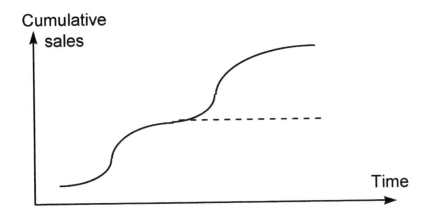

Figure 5.7   *Stair-pattern diffusion curve*

customers need before they forge an opinion of the product and communicate their reactions to the salespeople. Sales can pick up from there if the feedback is favourable, or stay as they were, if otherwise.

In volume-orientated markets, your salesforce and your marketing function have to weave a close network. They need to visit more and more prospects, systematically contact all people concerned and, at the same time, make sure these contacts are increasingly varied (customers, experts, advisors). This will help to publicize your business and establish links between the different protagonists so that you end up by building a specific network for your innovation. It's an important operation because in fact the new product is going to be diffused within this same network. Now is the right time to contact distributors if the product needs to go via such people. All things considered, a network is one of the best communication supports to be found for promoting a technological innovation. According to Abratt (1986), the most that advertising, mailing, telephoning and reply coupons can achieve is to inform clients that a product exists. On the other hand, shows, visits and especially the grapevine are incomparably efficient at convincing customers to buy. Which all goes to back up MacKenna's (1991) faith in hearsay. Abratt (1986) adds that clients need to have a face-to-face meeting with suppliers if the outcome is to be concrete. For one thing, clients should have the opportunity to talk about techniques with suppliers and, for another thing, to hear the advice of a third party who has already used the product.

The mesh effect of a network like this is a guarantee of success because it provides diffusion channels for the innovation. The mesh is like a preliminary wiring up. Sometimes it amounts to only a few contacts when the market is very concentrated or when production is geared to one privileged customer. You can liken this socio-economic mesh to the technical mesh effect used in a niche strategy. For example, the team that was running the reinforcement fibre project signed a contract at this stage with a large building and public works company concerning concrete for use at sea, a contract with prefabricated concrete manufacturers, a contract with a company who resurfaced roads, a contract with an international technical water centre and a big provincial city, a contract with a national power utility to promote the use of the product in concrete drains and piping, and a contract with people who made cement for industrial paving.

Reinforcing Information Systems

One of the essential points in a volume strategy is to create or consolidate your information system. This should be based on your segmentation and diagnosis; not the other way round. For instance, once you have identified a segment composed of highly polluting chemical factories, you need to track them down and hunt them out. You procure a directory of polluted sites from the environmental ministry and a list of the participants at the Pollutech show... This is also the right time to enrich and validate your segmentation. Lastly, companies that created a "watch" during the diagnosis phase should make it operational and keep a closer eye on sensitive areas.

What's more, this is the stage of the project when your product's future is played out. So it is fundamental to be even more vigilant with your first customers, ensure you get any feedback immediately. That will leave you time to correct errors. During this phase it's also important to check that you have reached the results you hoped for on your specific targets, and to watch out for new self-determining targets that might appear. Similarly, if your results fall short of targets, you have to try to understand the causes, just as you need to understand why some new potential customers have become interested in your innovation quite out of the blue. In fact, surprise motivation like this can be found with other customers, too, customers who are that much easier to convince, customers who make choice targets just because their demand is a spontaneous demand.

Finally, you should seek to fine-tune your knowledge of competitors by obtaining information directly from customers when you're working with them, or by systematically answering calls for tender in order to align yourself with competition.

Communication

By definition, a technological innovation is not just the servile copy of an existing product. There's always a risk involved in launching. Experience shows that advertising should be handled with some caution. You must be sure of your product before you make any large-scale communications. As the head of the heat-transfer fluid project was quick to point out: "You don't advertise until you are 100% sure of your techniques. It's out of the question to crashland at the start for technical reasons. That could be fatal." In some cases paid articles in specialized industrial reviews can play a role in publicizing your product. However, this kind of publicity isn't generally thought to have a miracle effect, because it sometimes causes problems. If your team is reduced prior to selling it won't necessarily be equipped to keep up with a lot of requests for information. Then the rest of your organization will grind to a halt.

So companies tend to prefer direct communications like fairs, shows or visits. These have a much stronger influence on clients' purchase decisions and are much more controllable as far as after-effects go.

Abratt's (1986) statistics support all this and indicate that advertising can make people aware of your innovation, but doesn't make them buy it. The upshot is different when customers actually meet suppliers face-to-face and negotiate about technology. In half of those cases they decide to buy.

Communications are essentially made through your network. Most of them are related to technique and give quite ample instruction data. However, highly competitive, highly innovative industries may organize big launching operations with press coverage where they officially demonstrate the product. Journalists and customers are invited to a presentation where company specialists (like the project leader or the product manager) vaunt the product's features and performance levels.

Planning

This is one side to launching new products that most professionals in industrial marketing master well, as long as they use good checklists of all the elements and systematic tasks required. Particularly important elements to remember are as follows:

- Having advertising booklets designed and printed
- Having technical bulletins drawn up and printed. They need to be written in the relevant language (i.e. that of the country you're selling to), and should include a users' manual and maintenance guide. They should also be clear and brief, so don't have them written by the technicians who designed the product. There's always a tendency to complicate things when you want to explain it all
- Negotiating stocks with the production department
- Storage location: factory stock, stock for distribution, demonstration stock for vendors, stocks of spare parts for repairs
- Sales administration
- Aftersales service, including training and setting up a specific maintenance network for the innovation.

The measuring computer project is a good illustration of how careful you must be here. Shortly after launching the computer, the company was submerged by calls from customers who needed their machines debugged. The company had to instal a hot line and a 24-hour non-stop service in order to cope.

So putting a product on the market when you have chosen a volume strategy isn't something you can improvize. There are competitors lurking near, good professionals who could easily exploit your slightest weakness. One thing you have to be particularly vigilant about is launch lead times. It could be cut-throat to announce that your product will be shortly appearing and then bring it out a year later. This is not a consumer market where announcements made ahead of time might pay off sales-wise because they stimulate customer expectancy and interest. In the present case, clients will put off buying until they can't wait any longer, then they will order from your competitors. And most of the time this type of purchase is irrevocable. That is, a customer who buys an oscilloscope from competition isn't likely to buy a second one from you just to make you happy. This kind of dysfunction soon doubles or quadruples your launch costs. So make sure that your prototypes and the initial production batch are finished first. Keeping to procedures and to your launch plan is obviously crucial when you launch a product on volume-orientated markets. One little cog in the wheel (like stocks that don't arrive) can jam a whole process and wreck all the efforts behind it.

A CONDENSED COMPARISON OF THE TWO STRATEGIES

Table 5.2 can be used to sum up comparisons between a niche strategy and a volume strategy. We will successively compare the characteristics of both strategies, the steps to take in each case and success factors.

The value of having identified these two types of strategy becomes self-evident when you choose between them. It's obvious that you won't be able to make quick inroads into volume-orientated markets when you're applying the rules for niches. But there's still one question: on what criteria do you base either strategy? We have gleaned four empirical rules of action just by observing a lot of successful launches:

- You use a volume strategy when there's a market available for mass-produced or continuous process products.
- You generally use a volume strategy when your company has a volume culture (i.e. is used to making large quantities at low cost) and doesn't foresee any big changes in its activity.
- You generally use a niche strategy when your technology has no known equivalent (i.e. it implies an entirely new vision of things and new ways of working...).
- You should use a niche strategy when the people promoting

Table 5.2   *A condensed comparison of niche and volume strategies*

	Niche strategy	Volume strategy
Characteristics	• To make maximum profits from technical features • To surpass existing technology • To saturate small high-tech segments one by one • To build the market from scratch • Accepted once it is an accomplished fact	• To seek volume to offset costly investments • To have competitive advantage over comparable technologies • To attack markets already served by competitors • To substitute for existing markets by taking large market shares (above 30% if possible, not below 15%) • Often imposed by shareholders or management for immediate profitability
Steps to take	• Co-develop with technically orientated clients to meet an acute technical problem • Use segments as intermediary goals to acquire experience and references necessary for more important segments • Be geared to answers rather than products • Sell a brand-new concept at price unrelated to cost price	• Co-develop with strongly motivated lead users • Adjust offer carefully to customer requirements; be ready to mask superfluous features • Launch directly on big markets with purchase-orientated, risk-sensitive clients • Analyse marketing situation carefully to respect market constraints • Be geared to products rather than answers • Sell product, performance, quality, service at a predefined price
Seeds for success	• Respect offer–need dialectic in business growth plan • Develop with a partner • Set up technical support web • Create adapted technical set-up if immediate insertion of technology unfeasible	• Analyse market rigorously • Respect procedure and launch plan • Set up commercial support web

your product are research teams trying to sell performance and technology, because technicians are better armed to sell technology to other technicians than products to buyers.

One final point to stress again about these two approaches is that they can work in parallel, to complement each other or in synergy. It's quite possible for innovators to start off with one strategy then switch to the other or use both in parallel, provided they're aware of what they are doing and don't apply the wrong approach to their situation.

Checklist

- You can use two complementary strategies to develop markets for your technological innovation. The first launch strategy consists of penetrating niches with the unique technical solution to a specific problem. Competition is limited here, so you try to take the biggest market shares possible by highlighting your offer's potential. The second strategy is a substitution strategy. It's also called a volume strategy because your goal here is to reach a certain sales volume quickly by snatching shares from competitors as fast as possible. When you choose this strategy, you need to know exactly how you stand versus competition so you know what tactics to use against it.
- Customer behaviour is fundamental in determining what action to take within the framework of these two strategies. In one case, clients are dissatisfied with the present offer and in the other they are not. Potential customers in niches are said to be technically orientated. They are plagued on a daily basis by an acute, recurring technical problem and seek a solution at any cost. They are usually job competent, like talking about technology and will be keen to collaborate with suppliers. This is the type of customer who likes meeting technicians. The clients you target with a volume strategy are said to be purchase-orientated. They are usually pleased with what they use now and don't see any reason whatsoever for dropping their current product and adopting a new one, because they seek to avoid risk at all cost.

Suppliers are generally handled by their purchasing depart-
ments and all new suppliers and new products are filtered
by a series of procedures and predefined evaluation grids.
- A niche strategy should be chosen when:
  - Your technology has no equivalent (i.e. it involves having
    an entirely new vision of things and a new way of
    working)
  - Research or development teams are promoting the
    innovation, so in fact what you are trying to sell is
    performance and technology. Technicians are better at
    selling technology to fellow-technicians than products to
    buyers.
- A volume strategy should be chosen when:
  - There's a market available for mass-produced or contin-
    uous process products
  - Your company has a strong volume culture (i.e. it's used
    to making very large quantities at low cost) and doesn't
    intend to diverge much from what it usually does.

REFERENCES

Abernathy, W. and Utterback, J. (1978). Patterns of industrial
innovations. *Innovation/Technology Review*.

Abratt, R. (1986). Industrial buying in high-tech markets. *Industrial
Marketing Management*, No. 15.

Asimov, I. (1960). *Foundation*. London: Panther.

Davidow, W.H. (1986). *Marketing High Technology – An Insider's View*.
New York: The Free Press.

Detoeuf, A. (1989). *Propos de O.L. Barenton, confiseur*. Paris: Editions
d'Organisation. First edition 1982 by Editions du Tambourinaire.

Green, K. (1991). Shaping markets: Creating demand for radically new
products. *Actes du colloque: Management of technology: implications for
enterprise management and public policy*. Paris.

Hamel, G. and Prahalad, C.K. (1992). Sept idées pour découvrir de
nouveaux marchés. *Harvard l'Expansion*, Spring.

MacKenna, R. (1991). Marketing is everything. *Harvard Business
Review*, January–February.

Salle, R. and Silvestre, H. (1992). *Vendre à l'industrie.* Paris: Editions de Liaison.

Turnbull, P. and Valla, J.-P. (1986). *Strategies for International Industrial Marketing.* London: Croom Helm.

6
Building Up Your Business

Whether you choose a niche strategy or a volume strategy, you have to establish a plan. Broadly speaking, that means deciding which segments you intend to penetrate, in what order, with what product and how. However, there are some specific points to remember when you plan to develop business around an innovation. They can be summed up in four general rules:

- Launch your offensive on the less important segments. View these so-called "access" segments as intermediary marketing objectives.
- Capitalize on what you gain in the first segments. This will help you to attack the bigger segments you aim to develop.
- Secure your position before you go for any new segments.
- Keep your growth in line with your means and your ambitions.

RULES FOR MAKING YOUR PLAN OF ATTACK

Fixing Intermediary Objectives

The first rule for your plan of attack is to set yourself midway goals instead of rushing in to tackle large attractive markets that you can target later on. We shall refer to these initial objectives as access segments or intermediary segments. Intermediary segments are far from being El Dorado, but they represent very little technical and commercial risk on a short-term basis. When you choose these first segments you are taking that "easy way out" which makes you go where success is least hard to reap. And in fact you have relatively high chances of succeeding here. There are several advantages to intermediary segments. For one thing, initial success boosts the morale and allays fears of failure. As they say in combat marketing: if you want to win the war, you have to win the fights first. And for another thing, these access segments are a real gateway to more important segments. They provide the opportunity for full-scale experiments, help you to make progress with your clientele, to get to know the market and find out how it works. Basically, they are a way to improve your hand at the market without endangering your company if you fail, since any possible failure would be comparatively insignificant. In fact they amount to a sort of training process. Mistakes are still forgiven here, because any publicity made about you will be limited to small, quite insular segments.

De Maricourt (1994) once described the Japanese approach this way: "They rarely go in for direct onslaught because that's always heavy on resources. They prefer more oblique strategy, 'by the corners' as Musashi put it. So Western management tends to underestimate the size of the threat." He illustrates this indirect attack strategy with an example from the 1960s, when Japanese marketeers conquered the American TV market by edging in with small, low-range portable TV sets into niches that didn't interest American manufacturers because they weren't sufficiently profitable.

In short, an intermediary segment that's chosen with a view to attacking other markets should enable you to ride in on the wave. Small segments like this don't imply too much expenditure and they aren't risky. The real benefit you get from these midway goals is obviously not pecuniary but qualitative, and you can evaluate it in terms of acquired competence that will serve in offensives later on. It's crucial to abide by this basic rule in access markets if you want to build up your business on solid foundations, but unfortunately it's still quite an uncommon reflex with managers, especially managers of large companies. Peters (1988) underlines the fact that it's impossible to interest the president of a company that's worth $5 billion in a $100 000 market for scissor-blades or hand-razors. And he quotes L. Rivers, planning director for Allied Signal, who said that his company was going to go straight for ceramic (car) engines, that it refused to do a training period on the little markets first. What can you say to that?

In the composite material project, the company systematically chose low-risk, high-tech segments and renounced all attempts on high-risk segments over a short-term period. There were two reasons behind this. First, the high-tech segments represented small volumes that were compatible with the size of their pilot production units. Second, they were essentially composed of army representatives who were ready to invest time and money in developing components, while a more "civilian" version of these would suit the big electrotechnical market. But what the customers on the electrotechnical market wanted was a perfect product in large quantities and at low cost. And this wasn't feasible until the product had reached the industrial stage, after all the development problems had been hammered out with the army.

Access Segments in Niches

Access segments in niches are obviously going to be technically orientated. Customers here are beset by apparently insurmountable technical problems that they would give anything to solve. This is why they agree to collaborate with suppliers to develop adequate answers. Innovators are then able to build up their capital in technology on the basis of this co-development with the users, and accede to other market segments by dint of knowledge, experience and references.

Facing up to demanding clients also makes you progress a lot in fields that are related, or complementary, to your product. Customers may demand improvements in quality, control, norms, industrialization. These are all necessary factors that you would usually have dealt with later on.

Finally, technically orientated customers help you to acquire usable references on other market segments. They are instrumental too in the discovery of other potential applications. And these applications are often very relevant to the innovations because the customers themselves are spontaneously defining what they want here.

But you have to go beyond the customers if you're thinking in terms of market segments. Technically orientated clients are only really useful if they're representative and if there is a certain number of them in the same market segment. So the first task after segmentation is to count the customers who correspond to segment definition. This operation will tell you whether segments are empty, small, medium-sized or vast, and how to rank them in order of commercial and strategic value as far as you are concerned. Generally speaking, innovators choose small access segments (i.e. with few customers) that correspond to the limited number of prospectors they can afford to mobilize. In terms of business volume too, segment size is usually in line with the sort of production levels their development team can furnish.

The reinforcement fibre project had a pilot site on a large provincial city's main drainage system, and it was this unit that opened the intermediary segment on drain renovation. The market was very small, but this wasn't a drawback because production capacity was limited anyway. On the other hand, the team acquired an inestimable amount of knowledge from their experience here, and it was on the strength of this that the project was able to go ahead on larger segments. This is why these first segments are referred to as intermediary marketing objectives. They serve as stepping stones to bigger business in segments where the odds are higher.

Co-development brings excellent results as long as there is fair play and the rules are clear. It has advantages for everyone, except where customers feel they're just being used to iron out initial problems.

Access Segments on Volume-orientated Markets

If you're using a volume strategy, you choose your intermediary segments among the less risky ones from an economic and strategic standpoint. Picking second-rank segments is a way of saving your shots for later, not wasting them through sheer ignorance of how the market works. Intermediary segments can also be segments where you aren't an obvious nuisance to competitors, and won't be readily noticed by them until you have had sufficient time to bolster your ammunitions against possible attacks. Basically you must experiment discretely, out of sight of competition, then launch out on a larger scale when you're ready.

Peters (1988) gives an excellent illustration of this strategy when he reminds us that the Japanese car manufacturers first invaded Europe via Finland. They were able to experiment at their ease on that small, "invisible market", learning to adapt to the needs of European consumers. A vast offensive was launched on Europe much later after a long period of trial and error in the Finnish test market. He insists on the fact that people who start in a small way only go wrong in a small way and that small projects aimed at small niches are soon stopped and soon modified. Peters also stresses that pilot experiments don't cost much, yet they can be a quick way for success in your project.

Building Up Your Business Segment by Segment

Building up your business largely depends on how well you exploit possible working links that exist between segments. That means trying to make your investments as profitable as you can, trying to make them pay several times over. This is what you're doing when you amass expertise and experience in order to penetrate consecutive segments. Of course, there are exceptions to the rule. Specific investments in a single market are justifiable if the market there is big enough to mean that you will have quick returns on your investments all the same.

You progressively gain experience in access segments through contact with the first customers, then you exploit this stock of knowledge to woo other clients in the same segment. These segments are a better opportunity for your company (volume-wise, for example), though you will have to invest even more (in techniques, sales, information, communication) to get in, and teething troubles won't be borne quite so blithely here by the clients. This way, step by step, you use the experience you have gathered to reach increasingly large segments, building up your business as you go. To sum up, this is the strategy that gradually helps you into the big markets by skirting the risks, often high risks, that tend to waylay marketers in these segments.

The company behind the machine to make electronic substrate (CVD) chose a segment of small microelectronics firms making silicon wafers. These clients were technically orientated, as we said before. The company first co-developed a product with wafer makers in this segment, then they were able to attack another segment: the big Japanese silicon wafer manufacturers. The Japanese firms were making the same thing as the first clients, but they represented much greater potential for the suppliers for the following reasons:

- The number of machines needed
- The number of customers
- Their solvency
- Their large investment capacity
- Their loyalty.

These new clients demanded excellent standards, but the innovators had been able to review the functions and performance levels of their machine entirely due to their initial experience. And that reduced the risk of a rebuff in the second segment.

A little later, the company used exactly the same type of strategy in two other market segments. The first segment was composed of small companies making experimental wafers for optoelectronics. It served as a springboard to the next segment: big Japanese firms that actually produced wafers for optoelectronics.

The best example we have of progressively building up your business concerns a product called "cruciform" that was developed by SEPR (Société Européenne de Poudres et Réfractaires). The product in question is heat resistant, has high heat capacity, is very resistant to heat cycles in an aggressive gaseous medium and has a very large heat exchange surface. SEPR developed cruciforms to equip heat regenerators for glass furnaces. These regenerators are chambers filled by a pile of refractory material that's alternately heated by the fumes and cooled down by incoming air. The pile deteriorates because of mechanical heat stress and chemical aggression, so production has to be stopped periodically for its maintenance or renewal.

SEPR offered its cruciform refractory material to the big glass manufacturers first. But the big glass makers judged the markup

(× 2.5) was excessive for the uncertain results of a new product, and they refused. Then the company spotted some technically orientated clients among small foundries producing high-specification glass. These foundries had to stop production every three to six months to change their piles of refractory material. One of them was ready to pay any price to solve this major, recurring problem, and agreed to collaborate and help the company. They worked together on a test site. After conclusive testing, SEPR had easy access to other customers in this intermediary segment of high-specification glass foundries.

When all the initial problems had been solved, the innovators were able to reach classical glass foundries that had to change their material every year because of problems relating to the design and small size of the chambers. This penetration was possible because the company was able to prove that the chambers it had equipped in the first segment lasted three times longer in normal industrial running conditions. Factual evidence like this was much more convincing than any other arguments the innovators could have developed.

Then the petrol crisis came. The big glass manufacturers were now convinced by these experiments that "cruciform" was more resistant in time and had greater heat exchange capacity, so they finally agreed to test it. In fact it enabled them to restore what had been knocked off their profit margin since the rise in petrol prices. Once again, it was the full-scale experimentation in prior segments that swayed their opinion in the new product's favour. But these difficult clients also needed proof that something which cost them three times more really brought substantial savings.

Today, SEPR equips glass manufacturers worldwide with its cruciforms. They have been largely optimized since then and are now sixth generation. The company hit the big markets, but it got there via the small intermediary ones. The business gradually took on structure with the see-saw effect of offer and demand, but it also forged its own way through knowledge acquisition. This means that two different choices at the start can lead to the development of two different techniques, that these different techniques will give you access to different openings, and so on.

What SEPR did when they went into the small, non-competitive market of small high-specification glass foundries was to apply the same strategy as the one that launched the diesel engine. As Chadeau (1996) pointed out: "The diesel engine got its first markets where there wasn't any competition. That is, among bigger engines than the petrol ones they had at that time, and among smaller engines than the big steam or electric turbines they were using in heavy industry or steam ships." We know the rest. Thirty years later the diesel engine had invaded the railway industry. In 1939, 65% of the ships under construction had diesel engines. In 1995, 85% of all trucks over 3.5 tons were equipped with diesel engines and, on some markets, over 70% of the medium- and high-range cars ran on diesel too.

The growth of this business can be schematized as in Figure 6.1. The top part of the figure shows that attack on the segments tends to be sequential and that there's a transitory state prior to each launch, as seen in Chapter 3. The lower part illustrates the fact that a certain amount of knowledge and experience $\Delta 1$ is acquired with the clients in S1 during transitory state 1. It's used to reach the customers in S2. More knowledge is then gained with them: $\Delta 2$. This knowledge is then exploited in S3 and so on, until the last segment.

Figure 6.1 also shows that entry into S1 implies having minimum levels in the following: technical competence, knowledge of the customers, sales experience, references or image. When you go into S1, you gain a little in technical proficiency because you have to master new problems. You also acquire a bit

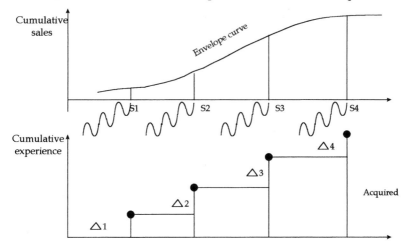

Figure 6.1   *Sequence form of business growth process*

more sales experience by trying out your arguments and testing customer reactions to offer. This stock of knowledge, experience and references adds on to what you had at the beginning and will help you rebound into the second segment. And so on.

The value of this strategy is to help you reach important segments more safely and economically. In fact, customers in these segments aren't ready to make any special investments so any development costs would have to be carried alone. What's more, you don't benefit from customer expertise when you're working on your own: your results can be very random. On the other hand, Figure 6.1 clearly shows that you make only a marginal amount of effort each time (Δi) if you follow the steps indicated, yet you end up in the most important segments because you build on what you acquire as you go along. In other words, this strategy helps you to important segments by avoiding the risks that are endemic there.

Ed McCracken (see Prokesch, 1993), president of Silicon Graphics, supports this basic rule of attacking in sequence. He says his company segmented their market rigorously, added on about one segment a year and created a new operational division to serve each of them and to focus on a particular category of customer and technology. That way the company was able to get more than a 50% share of the market on each segment.

Likewise, 3M,[1] who sell their products worldwide, recently extended their global networks to Turkey and then China, via Egypt, Iran and Thailand. 3M applies a very methodical sequential strategy when it attacks developing countries. Thanks to its wide product range, it operates at three different levels during the development of the local economy. It's initially active in the mining industry, then in building and capital equipment and, finally, in consumer goods.

Pilkington, too, use an incremental strategy to penetrate Europe, country by country.

> Pilkington Glass thinks that to remain competitive it's imperative they take a long-term strategic perspective. This is especially so in the glass industry, where major investments can take between ten and twelve years. They have developed a three-pronged attack on the European market. They are using their Finnish operation to ensure coverage of the European Economic

---

[1] See the article "Scotch fait de l'or avec ses inventions". *Capital*, January 1997.

Area and for building dialogue with the Baltic states. They are using their west German operations for penetration of eastern Germany, and they have set up a joint venture in Poland through their European operations. A focal point of the European strategy is the move of the company's headquarters from St Helens to Brussels. The Vice-President of the Polish and Finnish ventures is an integral part of the Brussels team, reporting directly to Brussels. As this indicates, the centre of gravity is seen in the industry as moving to mid-Europe. The American and Japanese competitors, through their European operations, have also set up operations in Hungary and Czechoslovakia (from Phillips *et al.*, 1994).

This business growth diagram is quite fundamental. It's a key factor both in your project's economic success and in the way you think out your strategy. The basic rule behind this way of thinking is to develop your business in sequence form by attacking segments one after the other. There are two essential reasons for this. The first is that companies always have limited resources, whatever size they are, which means they can't be everywhere all at once. The second reason is that companies can stray right away from their usual fields of proficiency and knowledge because of technological innovations. And they can lose too much time trying to find their bearings again to be able to attack a lot of segments at one time.

Right from square one, a technological innovation will be better adapted to some segments than to others. This is basically what determines your choice of segments in the short run. But once you have picked your access segments you will have to come up with more substantial ones that have real value for your company on a long-term basis. Of course, clients in these segments won't be much help in launching your product. They aren't ready to make concessions. They are in search of a product (as opposed to a technology) that works from the word go, sells at their price, and respects continuity of the materials and processes they're currently using. Before they make any decisions, they need references and that's why it's so necessary to have references already to hand from customers in access segments.

A successful attack also implies grading or linking potential segments so that you can class them in order of technical difficulty or value for your company. The grading will help (in part) to choose your order of attack on market segments. You attack one segment after the other and any rebound effect should be fully exploited.

During this process, the company jumps from one segment to

the next, acquiring experience with customers, using that hoard of experience and making it pay. This way, each new choice of segment is partly determined by prior choices (S2 is determined by S1, S3 is determined by S1 and S2...) It's a snowball effect that exploits any technical-, industrial-, commercial-type synergy to the utmost. But there are limits to this logic. It would be illusory to expect all the competence and knowledge you have gleaned on the first segments to serve on all the others. Some expertise will always be specific to just one segment and won't be used elsewhere, or won't be used systematically anyway.

In niches you look for any technical synergy that may exist between segments, as the market here is built on technical characteristics or advantages. If you try to solve different technical problems from one segment to another, you end up where you wanted, developing a coordinated range of products around your new technology.

In volume-orientated markets, you need to try to bring to light any possible sales synergy or industrial synergy between segments. For example, you find commercial synergy if you select segments that can serve as a later reference to clients in other segments. Selling equipment in a segment where they make banknote paper, for instance, could be a useful reference with manufacturers of high-specification paper. On the whole, any experience that helps us to sell better or to communicate better in neighbouring segments could be termed "commercial experience".

It's very easy to identify any synergy that exists between market segments by using segmentation and diagnosis. Segmentation, as described in Chapter 4, involves several criteria that can in fact be combined. These criteria explain the differences as well as the resemblances between segments. It's when you exploit these resemblances that you bring the synergy to light.

Let's go back to the example of the non-destructive ultrasonic control system (Table 6.1). The easiest segment to get to is S1, because it can be reached with an apparatus that's similar to the laboratory prototype. If the innovators get to S1 they will have mastered defect detection in metal parts using stationary measuring equipment. Going on to S6 is relatively easy because there's only one parameter that changes here: measurement input is no longer static; it's done by scanning. Once this type of data

Table 6.1   *Segmentation chart for non-destructive laser control*

Analysed material	METAL					COMPOSITES
System configuration	Portable	Stationary				Stationary
Measurement input mode	Static	Static	Relative motion	Scanning	Scanning	
Task required	Detection	Detection	Detection	Detection	Detection	Description
APPLICATIONS	Outdoor defect detection	Defect detection in hostile environment	Defect detection in parts in continuous motion	Defect detection in very large metal structures	Defect detection in composite material	Defect description in composite material
Data acquisition / Offline / Laboratory		S1		S6	S2	S8
Increased productivity / Online / Manufacturing unit			S4		S7	
Offline / Servicing	S5	S3	S10			S9

Buying motivation | Problem Location | BEHAVIOUR

acquisition has been fully mastered, they will only have to change one single parameter (the material) before S2 is accessible. Then, after penetrating this segment, they can reach S8 and go from defect detection to defect analysis. Any technical synergy has thus been exploited to the maximum (Figure 6.2).

In addition, you will see that when you go from S1 to S6, then from S2 to S8, you remain in research-type segments. Customer behaviour has been narrowed down and only the technical

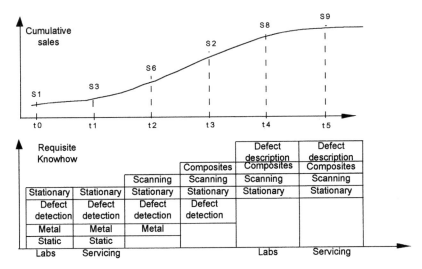

Figure 6.2   *Sequential development of non-destructive laser control business*

problems vary. As from now, we can anticipate future access to S3 (i.e. offline maintenance in hostile environments), which is more research orientated than production unit segments. The products offered in S1 and S3 are based on the same principle, but the product for S3 is more compact and more resistant to industrial conditions. Likewise, it will be possible to offer the same type of apparatus in S8 and S9, with respective versions for research and maintenance.

In Figure 6.2 you can visualize how business progresses in sequence. You find production synergy if you choose segments where you have the right amount of production for your production tool to operate at its most profitable.

International Factors in Segment Choice

Elf-Atochem had a specific problem when they launched their special watertight-but-not-airtight film for fruit and vegetable packing onto the market. The fact is that consumer habits vary significantly from one country to another. In Europe, the English are precursors in using clingfilm but the Germans wrap their fresh fruit and vegetables in paper. As for the French, they essentially use clingfilm to protect perishable goods in transport, but are holding out until European hygiene regulations are enforced before they generalize it to their displays.

Elf-Atochem's initial strategy was to attack the European market by co-developing with a French partner, which obviously simplified geographical connections and feedback. But commercial contacts were then established in Britain in order to set off the international process. The initial results were promising so marketing went underway with French customers. Now a little more time would be needed to overcome a certain environmentalist resistance in the German market.

The food industry is not, however, the only one where a specific approach is required for each country. In the automation field, for instance, developers are advised to attack Europe via a country like Germany, where PLC and numerical controls are widespread, rather than one like Spain, where electronic controls are in general rarer.

Securing Your Position

Basically what you need to do to secure your position is to concentrate your efforts on one segment until you overcome all the problems there, before going any further. The company who ran the reinforcement fibre project waited until they had solved all the implementation problems with drains and underground pipe networks before they went on to other segments. It was the same thing for the machine to make electronic substrate. The innovators ironed out their problems with small silicon wafer manufacturers first before they went on to tackle the big producers.

Securing your position also implies improving your sales. The further you go in a segment, the more people know you and the easier it is to convince them. Your sales figures progress too, which reduces commercial costs and increases your margin. It's worth trying to do as much as you can in a given segment, trying to gain the biggest possible share of the market, if only for that.

Strategically, it's of crucial importance to plumb each segment in depth before you go on to the next one. There are serious studies like the PIMS which show that people with more than a 30% share in the market have excellent chances of running their business profitably for a long time. This doesn't apply to companies with less than 15% of the market. These firms have no guarantee whatsoever of being able to keep on their business for any length of time. They only survive as long as they keep out of the picture, and appear harmless to competitors.

So this is why innovators must try to take over at least 30% of a small segment they are familiar with and in which they have a certain number of advantages. It helps them to master the game and control their segment well. On the other hand, it would be disastrous to plan on taking 2% of a big market just because 2% of a big market is enough to live on. You would be at the entire mercy of competitors and could be swept away at the snap of a finger. What's more, you have no control at all of the market if you just rely on luck to bring in those 2%. Your share is anybody's guess: it could be 1.5% or 6% of the market. First, customer reaction will be a complete mystery. Then you will find your sales volumes are only a quarter of what you predicted – or three times more, which means you won't have enough capacity to keep pace. That is, either your deals won't go through or they will, but customers will be dissatisfied. And whichever way it is, you have no prior warning.

This strategy is particularly relevant in volume-orientated markets because programmes like the PIMS are specifically geared to competitive thinking. Of course, a niche strategy is different on this point because there's no competition to speak of, or, if there is, it's not comparable. It wouldn't therefore be logical to restrict yourself to 30% in niches, since you're creating the market yourself. You should go for as much as you can. Why not 100%? This is quite possible, provided your segmentation is good, that is, if you've taken some care with segment definition.

For example, if you intend to launch into car manufacturing, it's better to say you want to get 100% of the small electric city-car market than to say you want to get 0.0001% of the car market. Maybe that comes to the same thing in terms of sales volume, but it doesn't mean the same in terms of commercial investment.

According to the PIMS, strong market penetration and co-development combine to make a profitable strategy. What happens is that when you co-develop you make a product that corresponds to customer expectations. This helps to raise customer opinion of its quality. And market shares and product quality are the two factors that best explain high returns on investment (see Figure 6.3). As soon as you've defined your

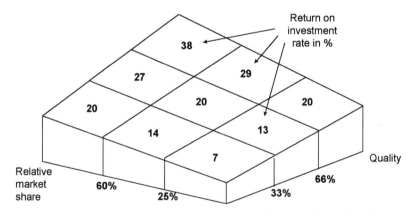

Figure 6.3 *Relation between investment returns–market shares–quality (Buzzel and Gale, 1987)*

segments clearly in niches, it's better to talk in actual figures rather than in market shares. The market share concept doesn't really make much sense here. You need to plan ahead in terms of tons or production units rather than in terms of potential market shares.

Keeping Growth in Line with Your Resources and Ambitions

There's one further advantage to attacking segments one after the other. It helps to regulate growth, makes it gradual, keeps your development in tune with your resources. The trouble is that when you invade markets your investments have to grow too, to keep in line with increasingly hard or stubborn technical problems, bigger markets, tougher competition. Davidow made a memorable comment on the electronic or computer industry when he claimed that to take a share in a competitive market you had to invest the equivalent of 70% of the leader's turnover.

Another point: your working capital requirements will grow in proportion to business growth, so it's really advisable to choose segments that you can tailor to your resources. Exponential growth is no better than a bad takeoff if you don't know how to control it or if you can't fund it. On the other hand, regular growth will help you fund your own development without any risk of financial problems, but only if it's adjusted to your means. In fact there's quite a simple logic behind this attack strategy. First, you go into the small unimportant markets where investment is low. Then, as more money comes in and you begin to fund your own business, it's possible to progress into more strategic segments where you have to invest more.

But quite apart from any financial aspects, what you basically need is a coherent plan of attack, meaning that you must bear in mind what your company wants to do, could do, or is really able to do, whenever you make decisions. These three decision poles can be schematized as in Figure 6.4.

What the company "wants to do" are its objectives, its intentions, its preferences, its culture, its company strategy. What we understand by "could do" is everything that we judge to be within the company's possibilities after we have weighed up

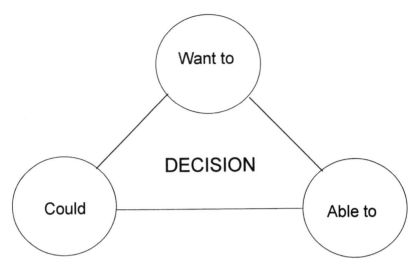

Figure 6.4   *The three poles of decision making*

constraints, environmental opportunities or market opportunities in particular. It's the marketing study that gives us the details here. Finally, what the company is "able to do" comprises its specific proficiencies, its means (i.e. financing, personnel and supplies) and its resources in general (e.g. expertise, support networks, allies, etc.).

These three areas influence decision but cannot be considered as dimensions because they aren't independent. For instance, a company will fix its goals in relation to an opportunity in the market and will be able to enter that market through some specific competence it already has. On the other hand, an interesting opportunity in the market can be an incentive to acquiring the necessary proficiency and resources you don't possess. It's all linked and the links go both ways.

FIXING YOUR ORDER OF ATTACK ON THE SEGMENTS

Investing in Different Ways

As we saw earlier, the order in which you attack segments depends on the synergy, or working links, between them. There are technical or commercial reasons behind this logic. And this is why we are going to progress by stages and build up on our achievements as we go along. Nevertheless it's impossible to pin tactics down to any general rules, because everyone has their own way of spending or investing money. It's partly due, of course, to our resources but also to more psychological factors linked with risk-taking, speculation, fear of losing, crisis, unbounded ambition...

The most you can say is that a given firm will be all the more willing to invest if the investments in question:

1 Are on a compatible level with available or accessible resources
2 Are revocable, in the sense that not all will be lost if a mistake is made.

A company that's thinking of going into high-speed machining may prefer to equip its usual machine with a high-speed spindle rather than buy a specific machining centre, because then it could recover its machine for something else if the high-speed system was dropped later.

3 Have synergy, that is, they can serve in several different segments.

For example, investing in a system to pipe concrete in its dry form could open up the following markets:

- Drain renovation
- Pressure pipeline renovation
- Tunnel construction
- Cliff reinforcement
- House-front renovation
- Dyke and embankment consolidation.

But this marketing strategy also implies that you have to base your choice of segments on certain criteria. It soon becomes obvious that companies have a mixture of rationally analytical and also very subjective criteria. More often than not, objective criteria seem to be used to dismiss segments, whereas subjective criteria frequently serve to justify a choice of segments.

Criteria for Dismissing Segments

One of the rational deciding factors is your diagnosis of the marketing situation, as we saw in Chapter 4. Segments in the very high risk zone should be left out for the immediate future, whereas it's feasible to launch in a market segment in the very low risk zone of the diagnosis chart. Thus you only select segments you're more or less prepared for, where market penetration requires minimal effort or is automatically accomplished as you go along. Of course, it's quite possible to gain technical proficiency and commercial experience in a segment while you're actually attacking it. You skip long weeks of preparation that way and launch earlier, well before you're really ready. But watch out for unfavourable publicity, and don't forget that some expertise and experience are only obtainable through contact with customers, the marketplace, and competition.

Among the objective criteria for leaving aside segments you will find veto criteria. As the name indicates, one veto criterion is enough to ban a segment, whatever the appreciation is elsewhere. No other criteria can compensate. There are three families of veto criteria used in diagnosis:

1 Marketing criteria
2 Technological criteria
3 Production criteria.

The following marketing criteria can eliminate segments:

- Longstanding proof that the market doesn't exist or that volume is far too low to ensure any profits
- A company's total ignorance of the rules the market runs by. Its sales organization isn't geared to attack, isn't present where it should be, or not in sufficient number, and doesn't know market rules.

The technological veto criteria are as follows:

- Totally inadequate technology: this criterion is enough to disqualify technology from a segment if there's proof that it doesn't, and never will, meet the performance levels required by customers. All segments like this should be systematically crossed off your list.

- Technology with a bad image: this means you have to face the preconceived ideas behind what's commonly known as "resistance to change". We have also seen that it can be an alibi to explain failure. But overcoming this type of resistance when you have understood the source can be very costly and demands a lot of extra effort.

Production-related veto criteria include:

- Patents that create obstacles: companies often give up the fight when they have this problem
- Production that's incompatible with heavy, costly production tools. (This is particularly true of volume-orientated markets.)

There are other cases of segment elimination that occur on the decision of new management. Or segments can be put on the long-term waiting list because of serious problems encountered implementing an innovation.

Another point worth making is that holding onto everything isn't possible anyway, due to the time factor and for financial and organizational reasons. So riskier segments are left out for the time being. In other words, you leave aside what you don't retain!

Criteria for Your Choice of Segments

The Concept of Bonus Criteria

Bonus criteria are some of the trickiest criteria to assess. They are criteria that mean more from the company standpoint and will swing the balance in a positive way. For example, the car market is a magic phrase for some people. It strikes the right note. As soon as some company managers hear it, then automatically, without further analysis, they tell you this is a better market – on principle and by definition – than the others. It's the car market, and that's where you need to go. And for other people this could be the food industry or the pharmaceutical industry or such and such a client. Everyone has their own particular hobbyhorse.

The concept of bonus criteria can also be explained by comparing it with the concept of veto criteria. You can't offset veto criteria, and any access to a segment under diagnosis is quite impossible below a given veto threshold. Bonus criteria, though, have exactly the opposite effect to veto criteria. Companies always prefer to go into market segments where they find bonus criteria with high scores, no matter how they evaluate the situation elsewhere. Mass markets, partners in industry or customers who are willing to co-develop can be bonus criteria because they are determining factors for companies in decision making. This visibly isn't a very rational way to proceed but March and Simon (1958) have already shown us that decisions are never in fact completely rational.

The thing is here that decision makers never have the money or the time necessary to inventory and evaluate all the possible solutions. So they tend to settle for the first solution that satisfies a few more or less implicit criteria they had fixed themselves. Their "rational" methods then consist of seeking out all the information that supports their choice even if this means neglecting or omitting the information that goes against it. It's what you would call "bounded rationality".

In reality, this bias translates company conviction that bonus criteria determine your success. As from here, the company is going to believe in its product's success, to show commitment and support. Internal barriers fall, the company pushes the project into chosen channels and gives it more chance of succeeding by so doing. In this way, a bonus criterion virtually reduces the risk entailed by a project simply because the company allocates more resources to that project. What's more, as we saw in Chapter 3, the mere fact of making a choice and focusing on it increases the innovation's chances on the chosen segment. And this gives good grounds for believing in bonus criteria.

Bonus Criteria in a Niche Strategy

There are three families of bonus criteria to be found in a niche strategy:

1 Technological criteria
2 Marketing criteria
3 Criteria linked to how the innovation is put on the market.

You can inventory the following technological criteria in this domain:

- The innovation brings a unique solution to the customer's technical problem
- The innovation is a breakthrough. It's the technical asset the company can exploit profitably in niches: markets where high technology makes the difference, markets that provide contact with technicians and give you technical relays to other markets
- The technology has a very good image. A good image is considered to be a very favourable factor that foreshadows advance sales. What sells here is high-tech.

We have seen the following marketing criteria in a niche strategy:

- Geographical nearness. This means that contacts are easy and any problems that arise can be quickly seen to. As things tend to progress rather slowly when you begin, domestic clients are looked on as an advantage at this stage because the language barrier doesn't create an additional obstacle
- Customer references that make a good showcase for your project and bring it to people's attention
- The possibility of having markups to cover your direct costs
- The inside impact of the operation. An initial outside operation that attracts a lot of attention will have a decisive effect in your favour within your own group. And, as everyone knows, that's where you find the trickiest customers.

The following criteria are relevant when you're looking at ways to introduce the innovation on the market:

- Customers who form part of your group are an appreciated reference because they're proof to outsiders of the confidence you have in your innovation. (*Note*: This can cut both ways, because it may be interpreted as manipulation.)
- Partners. This is the criterion that crowns all others in a niche strategy. Most successful companies launched their product with a partner who both shared the uncertainty and inspired confidence. Partners are either industrial partners or privileged customers. Privileged clients can be reference customers, showcase customers, competent customers who agree to collaborate, or clients with whom you have a good, longstanding relationship. They can also be motivated, demanding clients who force you to progress.

Bonus Criteria in a Volume Strategy

Veto criteria are more or less identical whether you have a niche strategy or a volume strategy. Bonus criteria are not. There are three families of bonus criteria involved in a volume strategy:

1 Marketing criteria
2 Production criteria
3 Strategic criteria.

The following marketing criteria can be found for volume-orientated markets:

- An established and reliable mass market (this truism won't surprise anybody)
- Moderate, and evaluated, competition. Competition is considered useful because it provides the reassurance of a reference system. It's a safety net. But it mustn't be too aggressive.
- Financially sound customers: this is obviously an important criterion for companies that want quick returns on investment.

You will find the following production criteria in a volume strategy:

- Fully mastered production, and compatibility with existing production tools. You have two choice criteria when you know how to manufacture and are not obliged to make other specific investments in production equipment.
- Compatibility with the customers' production tools. This criterion shows you want to be as limpid as possible from the customer viewpoint. It means you avoid disrupting your clients' production methods by maintaining continuity of the materials and process.
- The opportunity to load a production tool that's working below capacity: in some cases companies are forced to choose mass markets to saturate production tools that are running below capacity. A tool's survival may depend on finding that mass market. If the market isn't big enough, production has to shut down.

The so-called strategic bonus criteria found in volume-orientated markets are as follows:

- Synergy or coherence with your business: the way to minimize

risk is to keep to your speciality. It helps you to capitalize on your experience.
- A strategic sector: this is a sector the company aims to penetrate, or to save, if ever its business is in jeopardy. It would then be a condition of survival.

A PLAN OF ACTION FOR EACH SEGMENT

Basically what we spoke about above was the means needed to organize action over the market segments as a whole. By building up a general picture of the business like this we aim to find the best compromises, the best places to invest our resources in a medium- to long-term perspective. Now this general strategy has to be completed by deciding what action is to be taken to penetrate individual segments.

Basic Rules for Elaborating Your Plan

What follows is only really intelligible if you remember that you're in the heart of a transitory state here, prior to launching the product on the market. At this point you still have only a vague idea of the product you will be offering and the approach you ought to adopt, commercially speaking. In other words, you're still far from being able to launch a product and the whole point of your plan is to get ready for that now.

When you draw up a plan of action for individual segments, there are three initial conditions required:

- First, you must be able to give a precise definition of the offer you need to make and the sales strategy you need to implement as soon as the product is launched. This is the marketing objective to reach during the transitory state.
- Next, you must be able to give a detailed assessment of your company's situation at the date on which you intend to draw up your plan. This evaluation helps to see how far away you are from your goal.
- Lastly, you must be able to define what action is needed to reduce this lead-time, and reach your target as fast and as safely as possible.

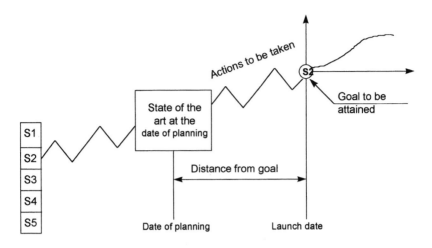

Figure 6.5   *Basic rules for elaborating a plan of action*

The process can be schematized as in Figure 6.5.

Definition of the Target

"Our plans miscarry", as Seneca said, "because they have no aim. When a man does not know what harbour he is making for, no wind is the right wind." It's essential to know precisely what your goal is if you want to be in a position to market your innovation. In the present case, there are three parts to the target we're defining:

1 The technical part of the offer (product, technology)
2 The non-technical part of the offer (service, price, etc.)
3 Sales techniques (your target contact, sales arguments, type of access).

There are three dimensions to the technical part of the offer:

- Specifications of functions, to define what the product does. This is product definition from a customer standpoint. It should include:
  - Functions expected from the finished product or from the process
  - Performance levels required for each function.
- Specifications that give an analytical description of supplies.

This is product definition from a supplier's standpoint. For a carbon fibre composite it could be:
- Composition of the matrix
- Carbon fibre ratios
- Presentation (e.g. roving or wave-style fabrics)
- Complementary components (e.g. decorative film, functional film).

- The manufacturing process and/or conditions of product implementation by the customer.

There are four dimensions to the non-technical part of the offer:

- The price at which you should sell the product. You should be able to fix prices according to your evaluation of the benefits customers get from using your product. We pointed out earlier that you could make this assessment during co-development. Obviously the price has to be above cost price.
- Conditions of sale:
  - Discounts (on quantities)
  - Invoice currency
  - Repercussions of variations in the exchange rate (especially for the dollar)
  - Separate billing, or billing with service.
- Delivery lead times: just-in-time, for example.
- The service that comes with the product: training, helpful development documentation, software, charts, help with setting or starting up the installation, assistance ramping up the production tool, aid in elaborating control procedures on finished products ... What we mean by service here is the service offered to customers who order according to standard conditions of sale. It doesn't include the (very substantial) service that companies provide during co-development. If the business is a service industry, then service refers to peripheral services around the basic service you offer.

Sales techniques should comprise:

- A description of your inside target. This is the person with whom you want to establish commercial relations: the member of your customer's personnel who carries company motivation for your product. For example, you may get in touch with the head of the design office who wants to go on to a new generation of products, or the marketing manager who's looking for a new way to differentiate. When the inside target isn't just one individual, you give a description of the buying centre (i.e. everyone involved in the purchase decision), with details concerning their individual motivation and power.

- Sales arguments to address this inside target (or buying centre). They should bear in mind customer motivation but also allow for your situation *vis-à-vis* competition. The implication here is that you can't establish real arguments just by brandishing the outstanding assets of your own products, whatever your ego says. Your arguments should include success factors. That is, elements you can count on to carry off a segment despite the present state of competition. This depends a lot on customer perception, because some characteristics can be overrated by clients in one segment and underrated by clients elsewhere.

- Who is going to distribute your product, and how. In other words, you must decide who's going to visit the customers if they are served directly. (For example, the project marketing manager will be in touch with the key accounts and salespeople will deal with the other clients.) If customers aren't served directly by the company, then you must specify how you intend to cope (e.g. through subcontractors, distributors).

- The communications you ought to make (i.e. the messages you should adapt for each segment according to customer behaviour and technical problems in hand there) and the form in which you should give them (e.g. booklets, videos).

- Your point of entry into the industrial sector. For instance, this consists of deciding whether you're going to sell raw materials (such as aluminium alloy slabs), semi-finished products (like aluminium bars or profiles), rough products (forged parts or cast parts) or finished parts (motor bearings, for example). You also specify which partners you intend to collaborate with in order to get into this market.

Assessing the Present Situation

There are three stages to making an evaluation of this kind (see Table 6.2). The first consists of a detailed review of all the factors that your marketing objective involves on each segment, that is:

- The technical part of the offer
- The non-technical part of the offer
- Sales tactics.

Table 6.2 *Procedure involved when invading a market segment*

Segment ●Name and brief description of segment ●Size and commercial importance of segment ●Technical risk level (✓=↘) ●Commercial risk (✓=↘)	Objective	Still to clarify: uncertainties to remove	Still to do: barriers to life, risks to reduce	Position *vis-à-vis* competition
Technical part of offer ●Functional definition (functions, performance) ●Analytical definition (supply contents) ●Process and implementation				
Non-technical part of offer ●Price and sales conditions ●Lead-times ●Service				
Sales techniques ●Commercial information ●List of customers, competitors, advisors, norms or sales regulations in force ●Target customers to contact and lead-users to co-develop with ●Inside target or buying centre ●Motivation ●Sales arguments ●Communications ●Organization ●Choice of point of entry into the sector and partnership (type of entry and commercialization)				

However, you may not be ready to define all these elements when evaluation time comes. For example, you might be unaware of the performance levels clients are going to demand for a given function, or what price they would be ready to pay for your product. If you see that one of the elements of your objective is missing, then you record it among the tasks that still have to be done – for instance, "Find out the right selling price". Tasks like this that help you define the various parts of your objective generally amount to no more than data collecting. They are said to reduce uncertainty rather than risk.

During the second stage of evaluation we try to measure the distance we still have to go to achieve the different parts of our objective. If you know, for instance, that the client wants the product to resist ultraviolet rays – which it doesn't as yet – then you add this development to your pre-launch task list. It would be risky not to reduce this discrepancy between your product and customer requirements.

During the third stage, you compare yourself (where possible) with established competition. It should be a good way to remind you where competitors really have the upper hand as far as customer requirements go, and where, on the contrary, you have a good chance of beating them.

Now your next step is to work out the position of the project on the target segment, according to Table 6.2.

The Action to Take

Certain steps need to be taken if you are to launch and to ensure steady, regular growth thereafter. The action you take depends on three essential factors:

- The kind of tasks that have to be done to reduce the distance between status quo and objective, and the kind of action needed to catch up with competition or to beat it. These tasks are listed in Table 6.2.
- The strategy used: either a niche strategy or a volume strategy. You adapt your action to fit the strategy you choose. Your action should be inspired by what we developed in Chapter 5.

- Marketing objectives in terms of desired commitment levels:
  - The market share you are targeting in this particular segment. If there is no competition, you mustn't hesitate to aim for the biggest share possible. You will have to specify whether you look upon this segment as an access segment (or an intermediary market goal) or whether you see it as a consolidation segment where you hope to obtain turnover and profits.
  - The annual increase in turnover you aim for in the segment and also your gross margin objective in this segment.
  - The resources to carry through your plan of action. A recently created company that's chronically short of money and doesn't have a commercial network can't expect to draw up the same plan of action as a multinational. You have to take stock here of all the tangible and intangible investments necessary, as well as your estimated requirements in working capital.

In fact, when you look closely at these three points, you meet up again with the three-pole decision: what the company could do, wants to do, is able to do (see Chapter 5).

A SUMMARY OF THE DEVELOPMENT PLAN

When you have decided in which order you're going to attack the segments (this is your general plan) and have found out what key steps to take on each segment (this is your plan per segment), you will at last have a concise picture of how to go about developing your business. Figure 6.6 points out the barriers that need lifting and indicates crossway links where there is potential synergy. The plan shown here is a richer, and complete, version of the growth diagram for the non-destructive laser control project (see Figure 6.2.).

You can visualize the action moving forward simultaneously in S1 and S2. The innovators are going for metal part control and composite part control as well. As it's much easier to accede to S1, they can look forward to launching product P1 in a year's time. Meanwhile, they're collaborating with a control research laboratory in the automotive industry to try to understand how

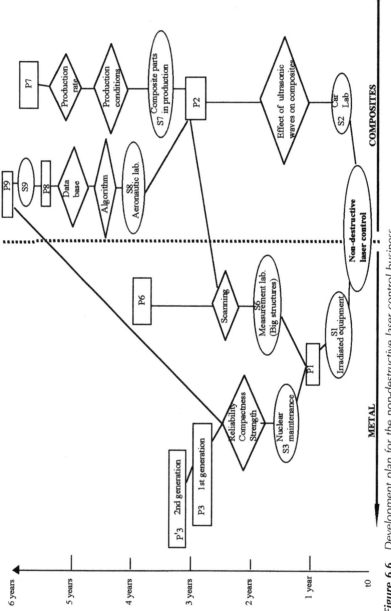

Figure 6.6   Development plan for the non-destructive laser control business

composites behave towards laser-generated ultrasonic waves. They can anticipate having a product adapted for this (P2) about three years from now.

Their next aim is to get into S3 (maintenance in the nuclear energy industry). This development has to be coherent with segmentation (see Table 6.1) and the plan for growth (see Figure 6.2). It will mean producing reliable, compact, robust equipment to go on the market in just under three years' time (P3). They will later be able to replace the first-generation product with a more sophisticated second-generation product (P'3).

In view of the relative positions of S1 and S6 on the segmentation chart, P1's success can help them reach the defect control segment in the big nuclear and maritime organizations (S6). But if they want to be in a position to launch P6 in four years' time, they will first need to master ultrasonic scanning. If you master the scanning process for metal parts, then you can transpose this technique to composites, which will make it possible to develop product P2.

As from here, the company can plan access to S8 (an aeronautic research laboratory) and S7 (control of composite part production). But this planning must be coherent with the segmentation chart and growth diagram. The innovators will then be able to launch product P8 in just over five years' time, provided they develop an algorithm for signal processing and create a database for defects. They could launch product P7 at the same time. It's a product that should resist severe industrial conditions and allow for high control rates. Ultimately, the innovators will be able to launch P9 in six years' time, thanks to the knowledge they acquired with P8 and developed in S3 to make their products even more compact, robust and reliable.

Checklist

- The following are the essential rules for building up business around an innovation:

  - Attack the market via the less important segments. These are your intermediary marketing goals. Midway objectives are more accessible than others so they give you an

opportunity to haul in your first successes. They boost the morale and help you gain the knowhow needed to attack more important segments without taking the risks you would have taken before. It all amounts to starting where success is easiest to find.
- Exploit synergy and build up on your initial acquisitions before attacking segments with higher rewards.
- Secure your position by grabbing the biggest possible market share you can before going into new segments.
- There are four criteria that help to screen your investments when you plan to develop your business:
  - How much you should invest to raise barriers. The more a company invests, the more it will have to try to rationalize this decision.
  - How revocable your investments are. The greater the risk is of losing your investment completely if you fail, the more cautious you should be.
  - Investment synergy. An investment that's beneficial on a large number of segments at one time will be all the more profitable for the company. The tendency should be to favour this kind of investment.
  - Returns on investment. You should invest more in segments which are more important and bring in quicker, bigger returns.
- The major economic advantage of combining co-development and market creation is a high return on investment. Co-development helps to raise customer opinion on product quality. Market creation is an opportunity to obtain large shares in the market through lack of competition. According to the Strategic Planning Institute, these two factors are the best explanation for high returns on investment. The following are the marketing components that you need to define and reach before you attack a segment:
  - The technical part of the offer, comprising product or service, an analytical description of it, its implementation
  - The non-technical part of the offer, comprising price, conditions of sale, lead-times, service
  - Sales tactics (target clients, inside targets, sales arguments, communications, organization, your choice of a point of entry into the sector and the partnership).

- There are two levels to elaborating a plan for growth. A general plan that consists of selecting market segments of the order in which you want to attack them and a plan per segment, which specifies the action you need to take to penetrate each individual segment.

REFERENCES

Buzzel, R.D. and Gale, B.T. (1987). *The PIMS, Principles Linking Strategy to Performance.* New York: The Free Press.

Chadeau, E. (1996). Une lente montée en puissance. *Les Cahiers de Science et Vie*, Hors série No. 31, pp. 82–89, Spécial Rudolf Diesel, February.

De Maricourt, R. (1994). L'art et la manière d'attaquer par les coins. *L'Expansion Management Review*, Spring.

March, J.G. and Simon, H.A. (1958). *Organizations.* New York: Wiley.

Peters, T. (1988). *Thriving on chaos: Handbook for a management revolution.* London: Macmillan.

Phillips, C., Doole, I. and Lowe, R. (1994). *International Marketing Strategy.* London: Routledge.

Prokesch, S.E. (1993). Mastering chaos at the high-tech frontier: An interview with Silicon Graphic's Ed McCracken. *Harvard Business Review*, November–December.

Conclusion

What do we retain from this book as it draws to a close? What does it borrow from marketing theory, and what does it actually contribute? Basically, it pays respect to one of the foundation stones of marketing, that is, the function marketing has of opening company doors to the environment. So it clearly supports the basic idea that marketing is construed from field data which you only get from direct customer contact. There's plenty of room given to intuition, uncertainty and turbulence in the book too, but it also stresses that good marketing strategy comes from systematic analysis and rigorous reasoning, logically and sensibly done. Segmentation is central to this analysis and it's an essential technique. But you can't expect your analysis to give results if it isn't written and presented in an intelligible way. This is why the book provides some logical, and concrete, rules to use when you plan to develop business around an innovation. These rules help you to ensure steady, regular growth, and to use your resources fully for any exploitable synergy.

Borrowed ideas aside, there are also some key points in this book that attempt to fill in certain gaps in marketing theory. Generally, this theory consists of analysing markets and competition so that you can devise ways to adapt your product as well as possible to demand and seize shares from competitors. It's a war and everyone's trying to improve their position in it. The trouble is that you need to have a position first. One of the characteristics of technological innovation or breakthrough innovation, though, is that it doesn't really follow on from anything. So marketing in this context is a bit like marketing in limbo. In a way you have to invent an initial situation that will give you some sort of starting point. But technical innovation marketing addresses this problem. It may be a rather vague starting point and you didn't necessarily choose it, but it helps to give some basic structure to your ideas. In fact, marketers tend to view new product development as a very linear and pretty irreversible process. For example:

- Product-idea or market-need identification
- Product conception
- Sample and test marketing
- Initial production batch
- Product launch
- Life-cycle management.

All this implicitly restricts your field of action to products that are already more or less identified on markets that are already targeted.

In contrast, technological innovation marketing admits there can be ups and downs, uncertainty, meanderings, chaos, turbulence. But it suggests another way. Far from trying to control what's reputed to be uncontrollable (and very unaccommodating for management), you should take advantage of it, ride out on the wave, even further than you had planned to. And then it suggests ways for you to ford this turbulence without seeking to control it.

The fundamental concept of a transitory state is therefore introduced here. A transitory state is that hazy interim period where the innovation faces up to its first customer problems but salespeople and marketers are still out of the picture. They either can't intervene or simply don't want to because the project fails to interest them. For the time being, it isn't only superfluous, it's quite frankly a nuisance. What's it for? Who's it for? Who's going to run it? How much will it cost? Where are the markets? Who are the competitors?

So the transitory state first reduces to sorting out the old R&D/marketing interface problem that so much has been written about. It's not surprising these interface problems exist when you have researchers offering electromagnetic wave generators and marketers expecting some sort of oven that dries plaster tiles quickly and economically. They're both in the microwave oven field, though they're not talking the same language and don't understand each other. But in fact these definitions reveal the value of the product from the client's viewpoint. It's another kind of marketing, much further upstream to normal marketing. And its job is to fit the environment to the project, so the project will be better fitted to its environment.

Second, the transitory state complements industrial marketing in a decisive way. Industrial marketing is geared to product flow management towards markets and essentially consists of running user/supplier relationships. The fact is that product flow or relationships are permanent state systems by definition. In other words, conventional marketing is perfectly suited to run established situations. The transitory state, however, is the converse of a permanent state, which is tantamount to saying that technological innovation marketing is there to help you manage the instability typical of fledgling businesses. It teaches you how to manage products that don't exist yet, how to approach and analyse markets that don't exist yet, and how to create relationships with clients you don't know and who don't know you.

Third, the transitory state is an investment phase, where you shouldn't only be making investments in techniques but in marketing as well. That is, you're still developing the product, but you also have to work on the price, on the service that goes with it, on how to inform people about it and the arguments to back up these communications.

The book also offers an alternative to a substitution strategy by suggesting that you can create markets or at least help to create them. The idea isn't new in itself, but this is a new way to go about putting it into practice. A comparative description of market substitution and market-creation strategies demarcates them clearly, and this distinction ultimately gives you a better idea of where you are. The book then goes on to indicate how you should proceed in each case, because the real danger here, in fact, is to choose the wrong strategy for a specific situation.

Bibliography

Abernathy, W.J. and Clark K.B. (1983). *Innovation: mapping the winds of creative destruction*. Harvard: Harvard University, Graduate School of Business Administration, July.

Abernathy, W. and Utterback, J. (1978). Patterns of industrial innovation. *Innovation/Techology Review*.

Abratt, R. (1986). Industrial buying in high-tech markets. *Industrial Marketing Management*, **15**, 293–298.

Achilladelis, B., Jervis, U.T.P. and Robertson, A. (1974). *SPRU Projet SAPPHO*, A study of success and failure in industrial innovation. *Research Policy*, **3**, 258–259.

Akrich, M. and Callon, M. (1983). *Innovations technologiques et procès d'accusation: les ruses et la raison*. Tapuscrit, Centre de Sociologie de l'Innovation.

Arrivé, A. and Millier P. (1992). *Analyse des états transitoires en marketing de l'innovation technologique*. Document Méthodologique, IRE 92, PHT.

Asimov I. (1960). *Foundation*. London: Panther.

Bachelard, G. (1983). *La formation de l'esprit scientifique*. Paris: Librairie Philosophique J. Vrin, 12th edition.

Baker, K., Hozier, G. and Roger, R. (1987). Supply-side marketing: risks and benefits. *Research Management*, 26–30, September–October.

Baker, M. (1982) Innovation – key to success. *Quarterly Review of Marketing*, 1–11, January.

Baker, M.J. (1975). *Marketing New industrial Products*. London: Macmillan.

Banting P. (1978). Unsuccessful innovation in the industrial markets. *Journal of Marketing*, January.

Beard, C. and Easingwood C. (1989) High technology launch strategies in the U.K. *Industrial Marketing Management*, **18**, 125–138.

Bell, D. (1978). Strategic windows. *Journal of Marketing*, July.

Bernhardt, I. and Mackenzie K.D. (1972). Some problems in using diffusion models for new products. *Management Science*, 187–200, October.

Bevan, J.(1987). What is Co-marketship?. *International Journal of Quality and Reliability Management*, **4**, No. 3, 47–56.

Bisio, A. and Gastwirt, L. (1979). *Turning Research and Development into Profits, a systematic approach*. New York: Amacom, American Management Association.

Blanc, F. and Molina, N. (1983). Recherchez de nouvelles applications pour des biens industriels. *Direction & Gestion*, No. 6, 15–29, November-December.

Bonanzio, J.G.F. (1988). The high tech market. *Industrial Distribution*, **77**, No. 9, 30–33, September.

Bonnet, D. (1985). Integrating marketing variables in early stages of the new product process to support the design and the development of technologically advanced new products. *The Quarterly Review of Marketing*, 7–11, Autumn.

Booz, Allen & Hamilton. (1971). *Management of New Products*. New York: Booz, Allen & Hamilton Inc.

Boss, J.F. and Tuvee, L. (1990). *Le marketing des entreprises de haute technologie*. ADETEM.

Bradley, F. (1991). *International Marketing Strategy*. London: Prentice Hall.

Brown, J.S. (1991). Research that reinvents the corporation. *Harvard Business Review*, January.

Burns, T. and Stalker, G.M. (1961). *The Management of Innovation*. London: Tavistock.

Bush, A. and Lucas, G. (1984). Guidelines for marketing a new industrial product. *Industrial Marketing Management*, **13**, 157–161.

Buzzel, R.D. and Gale, B.T. (1987). *The PIMS. Principles Linking Strategy to Performance*. New York: The Free Press.

Cadix, A. (1983). *Marketing industriel et innovation technologique*. Paris: ESC Paris, Cahiers d'étude et de recherche, 83–32.

Callon, M. (ed.) (1989). L'agonie d'un laboratoire. In *La science et ses réseaux*. Paris: La Découverte.

Callon, M. and Latour, B. (1985). Comment suivre les innovations? Clefs pour l'analyse socio-technique. *Prospective et Santé Publique*, 24 October.

Callon, M. and Latour, B. (eds) (1991). *La Science telle qu'elle se fait*. Paris: La Découverte.

Calori, R. and Noel R. (1986). Management stratégique dans les industries émergentes de haute technologie. *Revue d'Economie Industrielle*, No. 37, 3ème trimestre.

Calori, R. (1991). *The Business of Europe Managing Change*. London: Sage Publications.

Chadeau, E. (1996). Une lente montée en puissance. *Les Cahiers de Science et Vie*. Hors série No. 31, Spécial Rudolf Diesel, 82–89, February.

Chapelet, B. and Mangione, C. (1995). *Le lancement d'un produit nouveau*. Paris: Les Editions d'Organisation.

Choffray J.-M. (1984). *Le marketing de l'innovation*. Rapport d'un groupe de travail sur l'innovation, Grenoble.

Choffray, J.-M. and Akoka, J. (1980). La naissance d'un produit nouveau. *Revue Française de Gestion*, March–April.

Choffray, J.-M. and Dorey, F. (1983). *Développement et gestion des produits nouveaux*. Paris: McGraw-Hill.

Choffray, J.-M. and Lilien, G. (1984). *Market Planning for New Industrial Products*. New York: John Wiley.

Clugston, C.O. (1995). High-tech demands own new-product plan. *Electronic News*, 4 December.

Cohen, M., March, J. and Olsen, J. (1991). Le modèle du garbage can dans les anarchies organisées. In March, J. (ed.), *Décisions et organisations*. Paris: Les Editions d'Organisation.

Coleman, J.S., Katz, E. and Menzel, H. (1966). *Medical Innovation: a diffusion study*. Indianapolis: Bobbs-Merrill.

Compain, G. (1989). Les règles de la gestion de l'innovation technologique. *Revue Française de Gestion*, 140–149, March–May.

Cooper, R. and De Brentani, U. (1984). Criteria for screening new industrial products. *Industrial Marketing Management*, 149–156.

Cooper, R.G. (1975). Why new products fail. *Industrial Marketing Management*, **4**, 315–326.

Cooper, R.G. (1976). Introducing successful new industrial products. *European Journal of Marketing*, **10**, 253–329.

Cooper, R.G. (1978). Strategic planning for successful technological innovation. *The Business Quarterly*, 46–54, Spring.

Cooper, R.G. (1979). Identifying industrial new product success: Project new product. *Industrial Marketing Management,* **8**, 124–135.

Cooper, R.G. (1979). The dimensions of industrial new product success and failure. *Journal of Marketing,* **43**, Summer.

Cooper, R.G. (1981). The components of risk in a new product development: Project new product. *Research and Development Management,* **11**, 2, 47–54.

Cooper, R.G. (1981). The myth of the better mousetrap: what makes a new product a success? *Business Quarterly,* **46**, No. 1, Spring.

Cooper, R.G. (1982). New product success in industrial firms. *Industrial Marketing Management,* **11**, 215–223.

Cooper, R.G. (1983). The new product process: an empirically based classification scheme. *Research and Development Management,* **13**, 1.

Cooper, R.G. (1984). How new product strategies impact on performance. *Journal of Product Innovation Management,* **1**.

Cooper, R.G. (1984). The performance impact of product innovation strategies. *European Journal of Marketing,* **18**, 5.

Cooper, R.G. (1985). Selecting winning new products projects. *Journal of Product Innovation and Management,* **2**, 34–44.

Cooper, R.G. (1988). Predevelopment activities determine new product success. *Industrial Market Management,* **17**, 237–247.

Cooper, R.G. (1990). New products: what distinguishes the winners? *Research and Technology Management,* **33**, No. 6, November–December.

Cooper, R.G. (1990). Winning at new products: the keys to success. In Dorgham, M.A. (ed.), *Proceedings of the First International Forum on Technology Management,* pp. 213–225, London: Interscience Enterprise Ltd.

Cooper, R.G. and Kleinschmidt, E.J. (1987). What makes a new product a winner? Success factors at the project level. *R&D Management,* **17**, No. 3, July, 175–179.

Cooper R.G. and Kleinschmidt, E.J. (1990). The performance impact of an international orientation on product innovation. *European Journal of Management,* **22**, 10, 56–70.

Corey, R. (1976/77). Choix stratégiques en marketing industriel. *Harvard l'Expansion,* Winter.

Cova, B., Mazet, F. and Salle, R. (1992). Le marketing de projets; entre planification et laisser faire. Communication to *Eighth Congress of the AFM,* Lyon, May.

Cowell, D.W. and Blois, K.J. (1977). Conducting high tech research for high tech products. *Industrial Marketing Management*, No. 6, 329–336.

Crance, P. (1988). Marketing et technologies naissantes. Etudes de marché d'un produit très nouveau. *GMV Conseil* (document de présentation), November.

Crawford, C.M. (1977). Marketing research and the new product failure rate. *Journal of Marketing*, April.

Crawford, C.M. (1988). New product failure rate: a reprise. *Research Technology Management*, No. 7/8.

Czepiel, J.A. (1974). Word-of-mouth processes in the diffusion of a major technological innovation. *Journal of Marketing Research*, 172–180, May.

Davidow, W.H. (1986). *Marketing High Technology – An insider's view*. New York: The Free Press.

Davidson, J.H. (1979). Pourquoi les nouveaux produits échouent-ils ? *Harvard l'Expansion*, Summer.

Davis J.S. (1988). New product success and failure: three case studies. *Industrial Marketing Management*, **17**, 103–109.

Dean, N. (1979). Quels prix pour les produits nouveaux?. *Harvard l'Expansion*, 45-57, Summer.

Detoeuf, A. (1989). *Propos de O.L Barenton; Confiseur*. Paris: Editions d'Organisation.

Dorey, F. (1985). *Les facteurs explicatifs de la performance commerciale relative d'un nouveau produit industriel*. Thèse pour le doctorat d'Etat, Université de Droit, d'Economie et des Sciences d'Aix/ Marseille, IAE.

Dorey, F. and Valla, J.P. (1986). *La segmentation en marketing industriel*. Club Marketing Industriel RA, IRE, March.

Drucker, P.F. (1985). The discipline of innovation. *Harvard Business Review*, **63**, 67, May–June.

Duhamel, Y. (1971). L'étude de motivation en milieu industriel. *Vendre, Industrie*, No. 525, 3–7, October.

Dumbleton, J. (1986). *Management of High Technology Research and Development*. Amsterdam: Elsevier.

Durand, T. (1986). Les entreprises expérimentent de nouvelles stratégies d'accès à la technologie. Working Paper, ECP.

Erichson, B. (1981). Testing new products and assessing their chances. *Marketing ZFP* (RFA), 201–207, August.

Ford, D. and Ryan, C. (1981). Vendez votre technologie au bon moment. *Harvard l'Expansion*, Summer.

Fortier, Y. (1989). La gestion de l'activité de recherche et développement chez IBM: enseignement du passé et perspectives d'avenir. *Cahier de Recherche*, No. 89.12, CETAI HEC Montreal.

Foster, R.N. (1986). *Innovation: the attacker's advantage*. London: Macmillan.

Foxall, G. and Johnston, B. (1987). Strategies of user-initiated innovation. *Technovation*, Netherlands, **6**, No. 2, 77–102, June.

Freeman, C. (1988). A quoi tiennent la réussite ou l'echec des innovations dans l'industrie? *Culture Technique*, No. 18, March.

Gaillard, J.M. (1990). *Contribution à une théorie du projet d'innovation technologique*. Document de recherche IRE 9127, PHT, November.

Gaillard, J.M. (1990). *Le cycle de vie d'un projet d'innovation technologique: vers une nouvelle forme de typologie*. Document de recherche IRE 9128, PHT, November.

Gaudin, T., Bayen, M. and Portnoff, A.Y. (1983). Rapport sur l'état de la technique. La révolution de l'intelligence. *Science et Techniques*, Nos 97–98.

Gleick, J. (1989). *La théorie du chaos: vers une nouvelle science*. Paris: Albin Michel.

Gold, B., Rosegger, G. and Boylan, M.R. (1980). *Evaluating Technological Innovations: methods, expectations and findings*. Toronto: Lexington Books.

Gorge J.N. (1988). Stratégie de vision, stratégie d'écoute. *Compte-rendus du Colloque du Marketing des produits innovants*, Saint-Etienne, September.

Grawitz, M. (1986). *Lexique des sciences sociales*. Paris: Dalloz.

Green, K. (1991). Shaping markets: Creating demand for radically new products. *Actes du colloque: Management of technology: implications for enterprise management and public policy*, Paris.

Hakansson, H. (1987). Product development in networks. In Hakansson, H. (ed.), *Industrial Technological Development: a network approach*. London: Croom Helm.

Hamel, G. and Prahalad, C.K. (1992). Sept idées pour découvrir les nouveaux marchés. *Harvard l'Expansion*, No. 64, 78–92, Spring.

Henon, M. (1989). La diffusion chaotique. *La Recherche*, No. 209, April.

Hopkins, D. (1980). *New Product Winners and Losers*. New York: The Conference Board.

Huyghe, F.B. (1991). *La langue de coton*. Paris: Robert Laffont.

Iantsi, M. (1993). Mettez les chercheurs dans les usines. *Harvard-l'Expansion*, Autumn.

Jackson, B. (1983) Decision methods for evaluating research and development projects. *Research Technology Management*, 16–22, July–August.

Jacques, J. (1990). *L'imprévu ou la science des objets trouvés*. Paris: Edition Odile Jacob.

Jewkes, J., Sawers, D. and Stillerman, J. (1958). *The Sources of Innovation*. London: Macmillan.

Johne, F.A. (1984). Innovation in the marketing of high technology products. *Quarterly Review of Marketing*, 59–63, April.

Joule, R.-V. and Beauvois, J.-L. (1987). *Petit traité de manipulation à usage des honnêtes gens.* Grenoble: PUG.

Kapferer, J.N. and Laurent, G. (1980). Peut-on identifier les innovateurs? *Revue Française du Marketing*, No. 4.

Laban, J. and Morin, J. (1988–9). Inventer le futur. Les nouvelles offres technologiques. *Harvard l'Expansion*, Winter.

Lantos, P.R. (1989). Market oriented R&D. *Chemtech*, 152–155, March.

Latour, B. (1989). *La science en action*. Paris: Edition La Découverte.

Latour, B. (1992). *ARAMIS ou l'amour des techniques*. Paris: La Découverte.

Leonard-Barton, D. and Kraus, W.A. (1986). Comment réussir les changements technologiques. *Harvard l'Expansion*, Summer.

Lilien, G. and Yoon, E. (1987). La performance des nouveaux produits industriels, réexamen des recherches empiriques. *Recherche et Application en Marketing*, **II**, No. 3.

Lilvennoinen, P. and Vaanahen, J. (1987). Forecasting technological substitution, the logistic model of energy system revisited. *Technological Change and Social Change*, **32**, No. 3, 273–280, November.

Loveridge, R. and Pitt, M. (Coordinators). (1990). *The Strategic Management of Technological Innovation*. Chichester: John Wiley.

Lucas, G.H. and Bush, A.J. (1984). Guidelines for marketing a new industrial product. *Industrial Marketing Management*, No. 13, 157–161.

MacInnis, M. and Heslop, L. (1990). Market planning in a high tech environment. *Industrial Marketing Management*, **19**, 107–116.

MacKenna, R. (1985). *Regis Touch: new marketing for uncertain times*. Reading, MA: Addison–Wesley.

MacKenna, R. (1991). Marketing is everything. *Harvard Business Review*, January–February.

Mahajan, V. and Peterson, R.H. (1979). Innovation diffusion in a dynamic potential adopter. *Journal of Marketing*, 55–68, Autumn; (1978). *Management Science*, 1589–1597, November.

Mahieux, F. (1978). *La gestion de l'innovation. Théorie et pratique*. Paris: SIREY.

Maidique, M.A. and Hayes, R.H. (1984). The art of high technology management. *Sloan Management Review Reprint Series*, Winter.

Mangematin, V. (1993). Compétition technologique: les coulisses de la mise sur le marché. *Gérer et Comprendre*, June.

Mansfield, E. and Wagner, S. (1975). Organizational and strategic factors associated with probabilities of success in industrial R&D. *Journal of Business*, No. 48, April.

March, J.G. and Simon, H.A. (1958). *Organizations*. New York: John Wiley.

De Maricourt, R. (1994). L'art et la manière d'attaquer par les coins. *L'Expansion Management Review*, Spring.

Martinet, A.-C. (1983). *Stratégie*. Paris: Vuibert.

Masson, P. (1996). Confluences sous la mer. *Les cahiers de Science et Vie*, Hors série No. 31 Spécial Rudolf Diesel, 76–81, February.

Matlow, D. (1986). How to sell to high-tech top management. *Business Marketing*, June.

Maunoury, J.L. (1968). *La genèse des innovations, La création technique dans l'activité de la firme*. Paris: PUF.

McDermott, K. (1987). Selling high-technology. *R&D Reports*, 34–37, September–October.

Meldrum, M.J. and Millman, A.F. (1991). Ten risks in marketing high technology products. *Industrial Marketing Management*, **20**,.

Mendras, H. and Forse, M. (1987). La diffusion des innovations. In: *Le changement social*. Paris: Armand Colin.

Mensch, G. (1985). Get ready for innovation by invasion. *Journal of Product Innovation Management*, 259–265, December.

Millier, P. (1987). *L'interface Recherche-Marketing*. Document de recherche IRE 8706, PHT, January

Millier, P. (1987). *Processus de déroulement du projet technologique*. Tapuscrit, IRE, January.

Millier, P. (1989). *Le marketing de l'innovation technologique: Eléments pour une approche non-diffusionniste*. Document de recherche IRE 9021, PHT.

Millier, P. (1989). *Le marketing des produits high-tech: Outils d'analyse.* Paris: Editions d'Organisation.

Millier, P. (1989). Les produits à haute technologie – clarification d'un concept. *Gestion 2000,* April–May .

Millier, P. (1992). Mais qu'y a-t-il donc de différent à segmenter les marchés qui n'existent pas? *Gestion 2000,* No. 6.

Millier, P. (1993). *L'union chaotique du marketing et de la technologie dans les projets de recherche et développement.* Thèse de doctorat NR, Université Jean Moulin, Lyon III, February.

Millier, P. (1995). *Développer les marchés industriels. Principe de segmentation.* Paris: Dunod.

Millman, A.F. (1982). Understanding barriers to product innovation at the R&D/marketing interface. *European Journal of Marketing,* **16**, No. 5, 22–34.

Morin, J. (1983). *Management technique de la technologie. Réussite des innovations.* Note technique, May.

Morin, J. (1985). *L'excellence technologique.* Paris: Publi-Union.

Morin, P. (1980). Réponse au refus des produits nouveaux. *Revue Française de Gestion,* January–February.

Myers, S. and Marquis, D.G. (1969). *Successful Industrial Innovations.* National Science Foundation, 6917.

Myers, S. and Sweezy, E. (1978). Why innovations fail. *Technology Review,* **8**, No. 5, March/April.

Nash, T. (1988). Detecting a better market. *Chief Executive,* April.

Nehme, C. (1992). *Stratégies commerciales et techniques internationales.* Paris: Les Editions d'Organisation.

De Noblet, J. (1991). *Ruptures,* Art Press, Hors Série, No. 12.

Parkinson, S.T. (1981). Successful new product development: an international comparative study. *R&D Management,* **11**, February.

Parkinson, S.T. (1982). The role of the user in successful new product development. *R&D Management,* **12**, No. 3, 123–131.

Parkinson, S.T. (1982). Factors influencing user/supplier interaction in product development for high technology. 15th Annual Conference of European Marketing Academy, Grenoble, April, 454–482.

Peters, T. *Thriving on Chaos: Handbook for a management revolution.* London: Macmillan.

Phillips, C., Doole, I. and Lowe, R. (1994). *International Marketing Strategy.* London: Routledge.

Piatier, A. (1981). *Les obstacles à l'innovation dans les pays de la communauté européenne,* Commission des Communautés Européennes.

Piatier, A. (1984). Innovation dans l'industrie. Les enseignements de quelques enquêtes. *Etude CPE,* No. 32, May.

Pinto, J. and Slevin, D. (1989). Critical success factors in research and development projects. *Research and Technology Management,* January–February.

Porter, M. (1985). *Competitive advantage: Creating and sustaining superior performance.* New York: The Free Press.

Prokesch, S.E. (1993). Mastering chaos at the high-tech frontier: An interview with Silicon Graphics's Ed Mc Cracken. *Harvard Business Review,* November–December.

Quignaux, J.-P. (1983). Le développement des produits nouveaux au Japon. *Etude CPE,* No. 17, September.

Quinn, J.B. (1986). Innovation and corporate strategy: managed chaos, In Horwitch, M. (ed.), *Technology in the Modern Corporation: A Strategic Perspective.* Oxford: Pergamon Press.

Rabino, S. (1983). Influencing the adoption of an innovation. *Industrial Marketing Management,* **12**, No. 4, 233–241, October.

Revue Française du Marketing, (1988). Le marketing des hautes technologies, No. 117, March–April (Special Issue).

Roberts, E.B. and Fusfeld, A.R. (1981). Staffing the innovative technology based organization. *Sloan Management Review,* 19–34, Spring.

Robertson, H. (1973). The marketing factor in successful industrial innovation. *Industrial Marketing Management,* No. 2, 309–374.

Robertson, T.S. (1967). The process of innovation and the diffusion of innovation. *Journal of Marketing,* **31**, 14–19.

Rochet, C. (1981). *Diversification et redéploiement de l'entreprise.* Paris: Editions d'Organisation.

Rogers, E.M. (1979). New product adoption and diffusion. *Journal of Consumer Research,* **12**, March.

Rogers, E.M. (1979). *Diffusion of Innovation.* New York: The Free Press.

Rosnay De, J. (1975). *Le macroscope.* Paris: Point Seuil.

Rothwell, R. (1977). The characteristics of successful innovators and technically progressive firms. *Research and Development Management,* **7**, No. 3, 191–206.

Rothwell, R. (1981). Why a new product fails. *Marketing,* 29 July.

Rothwell, R., Freeman, C., Horsley, A., Jervis, V.T.P., Robertson,

A.B. and Townsend, J. (1974). Sappho updated – Project Sappho phase II. *Research Policy.*

Rubenstein, A.H. (1976). Factors influencing innovation success at the project level. *Research Management,* May.

Ryan, C.G. (1984). *The marketing of technology.* London: Peter Peregrinus.

Ryan, C.G. (1985). Innovative marketing – or selling seedcorn? *Electronics and Power,* 503–506, July.

Ryans, J. and Shanklin, W. (1984). High technology megatenets: 10 principles of HT market behavior. *Business Marketing,* 100–106, September.

Salle, R. (1984). *La vente en milieu industriel.* IRE, Colloque, 6 June.

Salle, R. and Silvestre, H. (1992). *Vendre à l'industrie.* Paris: Editions de Liaison.

Saporta, B. (1989). *Le marketing industriel.* Paris: Eyrolles.

Schroeder, D.M. and Hopley, R. (1988). Product development strategies for high tech industries. *Journal of Business Strategy,* 38–43, May–June.

Shanklin, W. and Ryans, J. (1985). Marketing et technologie de pointe. *Harvard l'Expansion.*

Shanklin, W.L. and Ryans, J.K. (1984). *Marketing High Technology.* Lexington, Mass: Lexington Books.

Silem, A. (ed.) (1991). *Encyclopédie de l'économie et de la gestion.* Paris: Hachette Éducation.

Simondon, G. (1969). *Du mode d'existence des objets techniques.* Paris: Aubier-Montaigne.

Smilor, R. (1991). The chaos of the entrepreneurial process: Patterns and policy implications. In Gibson, D. (ed.) *Technology Companies and Global Markets.* New York: Savage, Maryland, Rauman & Littlefield.

Souder, W.E. (1988). Managing relations between R&D and marketing in new product development projects. *Journal of Product Innovation Management,* **5**, No. 1, 6–19, 1988.

Srivastava, R.K. (1987). Marketing technology intensive products to industrial firms. *High Technology Marketing Review.*

Steele, L.W. (1984). Idées fausses sur la technologie. *Harvard l'Expansion,* Summer.

Steele, L.W. (1990). *Gérer la technologie.* Paris: Afnor Gestion (translated from the English).

Thomas, D. (1996). Treize décisions pour un nouveau moteur. *Les cahiers de Science et Vie*, Hors série No. 31, Spécial Rudolf Diesel, February, 46–61.

Thorn, J. (1982). Pricing new products. *Industrial Marketing Digest*, No. 1, 67.

Toffler, A. (1984). *Le choc du futur*. Paris: Edition Denoël (for the French translation).

Toney, A. and Tilling, T. (1984). *High Tech*. New York: Simon & Schuster.

Traynor, K. and Traynor, S. (1989). Marketing approaches used by high tech firms. *Industrial Marketing Management*, **18**, 281–287.

Turnbull, P. and Valla, J.-P. (1986). *Strategies for International Industrial Marketing*. London: Croom Helm.

Tushman, M. and More, W. (eds) (1988). *Readings in the Management of Innovation*, 2nd edition. New York: Harper Business.

Twiss, B. (1986). *Managing Technological Innovation*. London: Pitman.

Urban, G. and Hauser, J. (1980). *Design and Marketing of New Products*. Englewood Cliffs, NJ: Prentice Hall.

Urban, G. and Von Hippel, E. (1988). Lead user analysis for the development of new industrial products. *Management Science*, **34**, No. 5, May.

Utterback, J.M. (1971). The process of innovation: a study of the origination and development of ideas for new scientific instrument. *IEEE: Transactions on Engineering Management*, **EM 18**, 124–131, November.

Utterback, J. (1974). Innovation in industry and the diffusion of technology. *Science*, **183**, 620–626.

Utterback, J., Tuff, T., Meyer, M. and Richardson, L. (1991). *When speeding concepts to market can be a mistake*. MIT Industrial Liaison Program Report. The International Center for Research on the Management of Technology Working Paper 45–91, March.

Vagelos, P.R. (1987). *Managing invention and innovation. Getting more out of research and development and technology*. The Conference Board Research Report, No. 804.

Van den Ven, A. (1986). Central problems in management of innovation. *Management Science*, **32**, 590–607.

Van den Ven, A., Angle, H.A. and Scott Poole, M. (1989). *Research on the Management of Innovation*. New York: Harper & Row.

Varii auctores (1988). Intrapreneurship, entrepreneurship et gestion d'entreprise. *Gestion, Revue Internationale de Gestion*, Ecole des

Hautes Etudes Commerciales de Montréal, **13**, No. 3, Special Issue, September.

Varii auctores (1988). Le marketing des hautes technologies. *Revue Française de Marketing*, Special Issue, ADETEM.

Varii auctores (1991). La science du désordre. *La Recherche*, No. 232, Special Issue, May.

Von Hippel, E. (1977). The dominant role of the user in semiconductive and electronic subassembly process innovation. *IEEE Trans. Engineering Management*, **EM 24**, 60–71.

Von Hippel, E. (1979). The dominant role of the user in instrument innovation process. *Research Policy*, **5**, 212–239.

Von Hippel, E. (1982). Get new products from customers. *Harvard Business Review*, 117–122, March–April.

Von Hippel, E. (1986). Lead users: a source of novel product concepts. *Management Science*, **32**, 791–805.

Von Hippel, E. (1988). *The Sources of Innovation*. New York: Oxford University Press.

Von Hippel, E. (1988). Trading trade secrets. *Technology Review*, February–March.

White, G.R. and Graham, M.B.W. (1978). Gagnez vos Paris technologiques. *Harvard l'Expansion*, Summer.

Wind, J. and Mahajan, V. (1978). Marketing hype: a new perspective in new product research and introduction. *Journal of Product Innovation Management*, **4**, 43–49, Autumn.

Wind, J., Mahajan, V. and Cardozo, R. (1981). *New Product Forecasting*. Lexington, Mass.: Lexington Books.

Zarecor, W.D. (1975). High technology product planning. *Harvard Business Review*, 108–115, January–February.

Zollinger, M. (1984). Modèles de prix pour les produits nouveaux. L'apport de la notion de structure de prix. *Review of Financial Management*, No. 97, 43–60.

Index

NOTE: Page numbers in *italics* refer to illustrative figures in the text.

Index compiled by Indexing Specialists